D0579414

Grandmother's Secrets

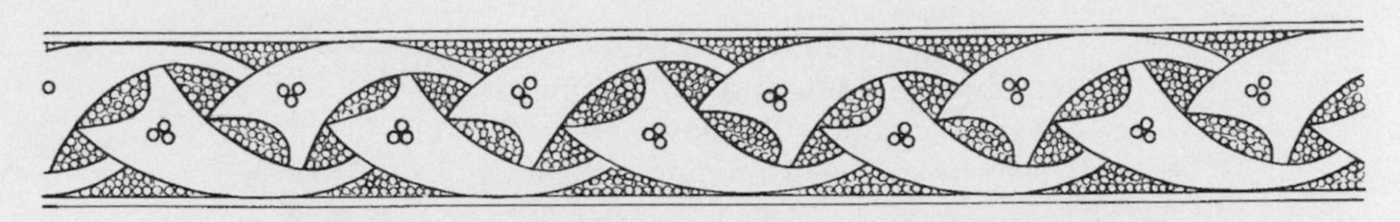

GRANDMOTHER'S SECRETS

THE ANCIENT RITUALS AND HEALING POWER OF BELLY DANCING

by Rosina-Fawzia Al-Rawi
translated by Monique Arav

INTERLINK BOOKS
An imprint of Interlink Publishing Group, Inc.
NEW YORK

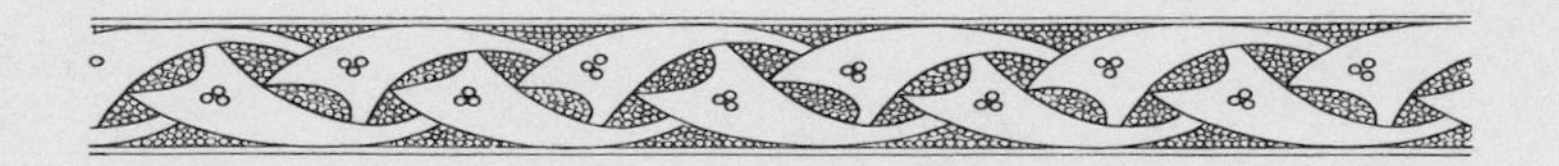

First American edition published 1999 by

INTERLINK BOOKS
An imprint of Interlink Publishing Group, Inc.
99 Seventh Avenue • Brooklyn, New York 11215 and
46 Crosby Street • Northampton, Massachusetts 01060

Originally published in German as *Der Ruf der Großmutter* by Promedia, Vienna

Library of Congress Cataloging-in-Publication Data

Al-Rawi, Rosina-Fawzia B.
[Der Ruf der Großmutter. English]
Grandmother's secrets : the ancient rituals and healing power of belly dancing / by Rosina-Fawzia Al-Rawi : translated by Monique Arav.
p. cm.
Includes bibliographical references (p.)
ISBN 1-56656-302-X (hardcover). — ISBN 1-56656-326-7 (pbk. : alk. paper)
1. Belly dance—History. 2. Belly dance. 3. Belly dance—Social aspects. 4. Al-Rawi, Rosina-Fawzia B. I. Title.
GV1798.5.A5 1999
793.3—dc21 98-38638
CIP

Printed and bound in Canada
10 9 8 7 6 5 4 3 2 1

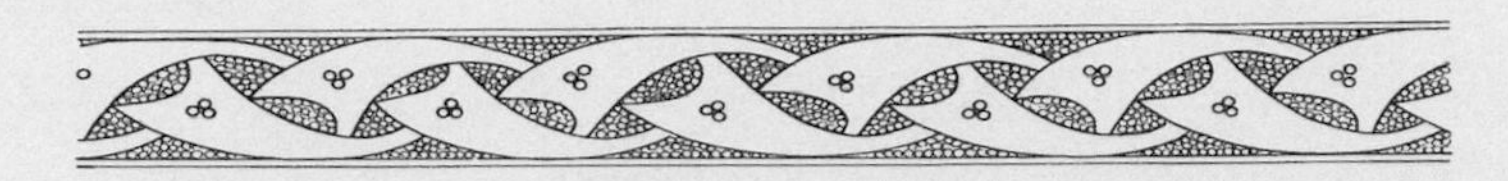

CONTENTS

PART THREE: FROM HEAD TO TOE

PART FOUR: VARIATIONS AND RITUALS

Foreword

A woman is the guardian and hostess of the earth. As the bearer of life, she stands closest to birth and death, thus closest to life and to the earth. This linking, life itself, is a woman's true space.

Writing a book on Oriental dance begs the question of where to begin. So many of my own memories are woven into this dance form that I need to go back to my childhood to form a full picture. This ancient dance form has long become a way of life for me, a symbol of my life consciousness. Much of what I have seen and experienced in my life has flowed into dancing. Dancing has been—and remains—a true companion through all the phases of my life. Everything I have lived and experienced as a young girl, a woman, and a mother sings through dancing. All the people, and especially the women, who have ever influenced me are brought back to my memory through dancing. The dance grows with me, while I grow as a human being and a woman. Every time my body calls me and nostalgia becomes overwhelming, I dance in that very instant, that intense moment of being. Each moment is different and each dance more whole than the previous one.

Belly dancing is an art and as such it entails three factors: theory, practice and the heart, without which no art form ever comes to life. This book is especially devoted to the first and third aspects of dancing, as they are often either neglected or totally ignored. As for the practice of belly dancing, it is shaped by each woman's personality, her intuition and creativity, the teacher being none other than life itself.

Casting a historical light on Oriental dance, I would also like to show how these movements, which have been passed on for centuries, affect individual parts of the body and the whole psyche. I want to explain their deep spiritual meaning and the purpose and healing effect of each of them.

One might object that belly dancing originates in a culture which is foreign to the West and therefore unsuited to Western women, yet this is precisely what makes it an even more enriching experience, apart from the fact that it is perfectly suited to the female body. By experiencing unfamiliar movements, a woman can allow her body to break through cultural norms. Learning this type of dance means learning new body wisdom and rituals, so that the dancer becomes physically aware of her culturally acquired conditioning, repression, and blockages. New worlds of awareness become accessible, releasing memories stored in the body and a joyful physicality that in turn leads to a less rigid way of life. Amid the jungle of confusing women's images, belly dancing can help women in the search for their own identity, as women and as human beings. It can pave the way for a process of self-awareness that helps them acknowledge and defend their own needs and wishes, regardless of sexual determination and the allocation of roles.

As I have suggested, the story of one's life as it is written into the body can be retold and understood in the intense moment of dancing. Thus belly dancing becomes a source of inspiration, a means of collecting and strengthening oneself, and a clear and dynamic way of discovering one's wishes and understanding oneself, no matter how insecure and doubtful the future may be.

Belly dancing teaches you an attitude: a new way to open yourself, far beyond blind imitation. It is a source of courage and inspiration that provides an opportunity to discover oneself on a deeper level. It is meant as a way to enjoy and a way to understand, and this all depends upon how it is learned and why.

This book is designed as a guide on the way to yourself, to new viewpoints and new conceptions of life, and to a deeper understanding of dancing. Its aim is to inspire you with new ways of self-awareness and bring you closer to your own body. Last but not least, it is intended as a bridge towards greater understanding and respect for women who come from other cultures.

This is how this book, originally meant to be much more specific, grew into the multicolored carpet on which belly dancing is performed.

When you read these stories, you may wonder how they relate to belly dancing. All these experiences are the threads which were woven into the carpet on which my grandmother let me dance for the first time. And she used all these experiences and thoughts to shape me into the dance, into my existence as a human being and a woman.

Since belly dancing mainly consists of circles, I shall start with a round dance, a circle of stories twinkling like a myriad of tiny stars filling up the great circle...

Part One: How It All Began

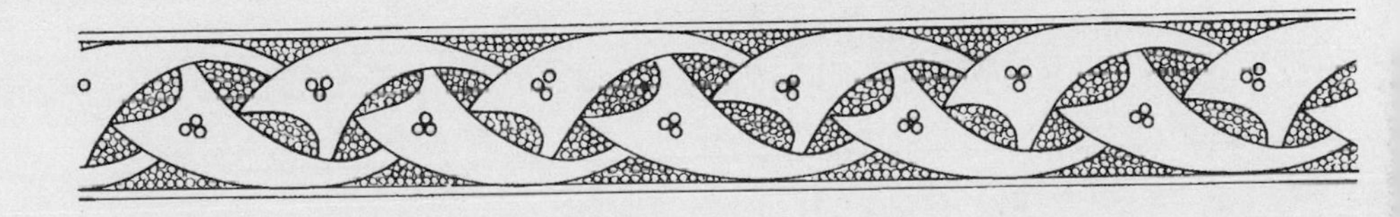

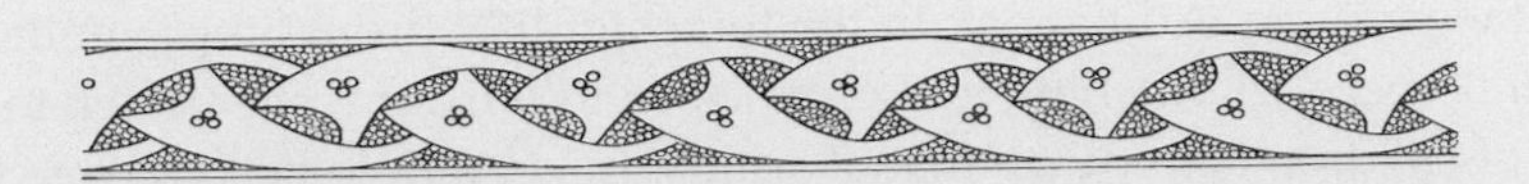

In The Beginning Was a Child

When I look back on my childhood, four characters catch my inner eye: my grandmother, my grandfather, and the two pillars of my childhood: Adiba and Amina.

We lived in a large two-story house in Baghdad, near the river Tigris. On the ground floor, a large corridor opened into rooms on the right and left, where my parents, my great-uncle, and I had our bedrooms. A huge common room, two storage rooms for food and other mysterious things, a guest room, a laundry room, and the kitchen completed the ground floor. My grandparents slept on the first floor, where my aunt, her husband and daughter, as well as my younger uncle and Adiba, one of my grandmother's cousins, all had their bedrooms. The official reception rooms were entered from a separate outer staircase, and whenever the sexes needed to be apart, the corridor was divided by a partition. Our common room stood at the center, and could be accessed from all bedrooms.

Amina, an old woman whom my grandmother had met by chance in a hospital as a girl, also lived with us. Amina had burned her face and her whole body with boiling water to the point of mutilation. Compassion drove my grandmother to bring her home and take care of her. Amina had no-one else in this world, so she just stayed with us. Such was the core of the family; in addition, our house was always busy with the comings and goings of close or distant relatives and many friends.

I hardly remember talking with my grandmother. Yet whenever she spoke, her voice enfolded me with authority. Her gaze was serious; her eyes did not miss a thing: she was a sharp observer from whom nothing could be concealed. Whatever the situation, she grasped it in seconds. She read people by their body language.

When I was a child, I respected her immensely, and feared her a little too. Whenever she called for me, I knew she had some kind of test in mind.

My grandfather, on the other hand, was the symbol of a great soul for me. His movements were those of a wise old panther. He was known throughout the region for his hospitality, and had reputedly been the best horserider of his time—no small feats in a society still influenced by the Bedouin tradition, despite today's sedentary lifestyle.

Adiba was a small round woman. Her eyesight was poor and since she was too vain to wear glasses, she would just screw up her eyes, which lent her face an odd expression. Adiba took in the things of life through her gentle heart. Her innocence was catching and came close to wisdom; she understood the world of children better than that of adults. In her ample bosom were buried all the family secrets.

Amina looked almost like some creature from another world. In her face, heavily disfigured by burns, shone two black dots barely recognizable as eyes. But woe betide anyone who paid no heed to those dots! If you took the time—and children know no time—to look into her eyes, a dark, endless ocean would open and take you into a world beyond the limits of humankind, into the elemental foam where pain and joy go hand in hand on a shore named being. Amina's body was so delicate it could barely carry those eyes. Wherever she sat, she would adapt her outer shape to her surroundings in such a way that one often missed her at first sight. Amina was the quietest being I have ever come across in my life, yet she carried in her the rhythm of the whole universe.

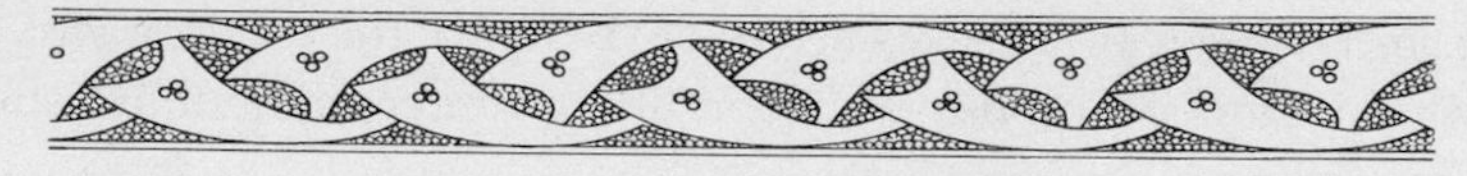

THE ANCESTRAL CALL

My grandmother would often watch me from the bench where she rested, sitting cross-legged. She would sit there for hours without moving while everyone in the house came to her for advice or instructions. She was a proud woman in whom dwelled an invisible force.

One day she called me. I came and saw a blackboard at her side.

"Come, sit next to me. I'd like to teach you an ancient craft. Take this chalk in your hand." She inserted it between my thumb and index finger and went on. "Now draw a dot and concentrate all your energy into this one dot. It is the beginning and the end, the navel of the world."

Time and again, I drew the dot, and time and again my grandmother told me to concentrate all my being into the dot. "Let it flow out of you, until you really know who is making this dot and nothing stands between you and the dot."

I didn't quite understand what she meant, and always drawing this simple sign really went against the grain. Still, after a while, I began to notice how my hand seemed to draw of its own accord and to keep returning to the dot. My thoughts disappeared and all that remained was the dot. I have no idea how much time had elapsed when I heard my grandmother tell me to go. "And come back when I call you," she added.

The following day, she called me again. "Fawzia, come!" She sat at her usual place with the board next to her.

"Now draw the first letter of the Arabic alphabet, the *alif*, a vertical line; start from the top, keep your hand light and put all your inner strength into the downward movement. Let the line become as long as three dots lying above each other."

Again, I took the chalk between thumb and forefinger, and I made an *alif*: ا .

She explained that the *alif* is the first expression of the dot. It is unique among all the letters of the alphabet and contained in all of them. Trace it with reverence, she told me, for the *alif* is the dot's longing to show itself. It is through the dot's longing to grow beyond itself that the *alif* is born. Regardless of their multiple, outer shapes, all letters are the *alif* in their essence.

How difficult it was for me to draw this simple letter! I drew it so often that in the end I could see *alif* in everything. Wherever I turned, it would appear. I felt my body straighten into a living *alif*. My arms, hands, back, legs, and feet all turned into *alif*. Like a matchstickman, I was down to essentials, clear and transparent.

Another day came when my grandmother called me. She sat on a bench in the garden, one leg folded under her, the other resting on the ground.

"Anchor your feet to the earth and balance your weight on both legs. Now shift your pelvis to the right and then to the left, as if you were drawing a shell. Every time you reach the furthest outward point, stop, balance back to your middle and then to the other side. Now come, make the same movement with the chalk on the board: ٮ. Does this shape remind you of something?"

"It's the second letter of the alphabet, grandmother, but the dot underneath it is missing."

"The dot is the beginning," she explained. "The dot begets all the other letters. The dot is below and the *alif* in between: ب . Together, they form the word اب (father), one of the names of the Divine. When you whirl or when you circle your pelvis, you are drawing the dot, the origins. From this shape all

My Grandmother

other movements are born—they all stem from this dot, from the navel in your belly."

I was excited to know that I carried inside me a source from which everything was born. Time and again, I watched the inward spiral of my navel with respect. Going around with all this power inside my belly made me feel secure and confident.

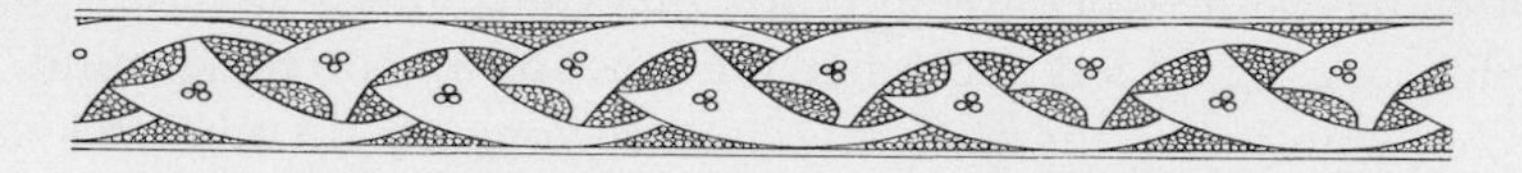

HAVE NO FEAR, SISTER

I used to observe my grandmother Fawzia, this fascinating woman whose name is also mine. She strolled through our house and although she was small, whenever she appeared, she filled the room. Her head, held high, rested calmly on her shoulders and her stance was always open and confident. One day I confessed to her that I was afraid to get up at night and go to the toilet, because it was so dark and far away. So she told me about my aunts and how when they were little, they had to walk out of the house, into the night, all the way to a distant earth-closet.

"During the day, try to find your way with your eyes closed, and you'll see that you don't need to be afraid at night. The difference between day and night is like the opening and the shutting of the eyes."

She often told me about other girls or women, linking me time and again into the chain of women. I began to feel I belonged to an invisible sisterhood that transcended past and future into eternity.

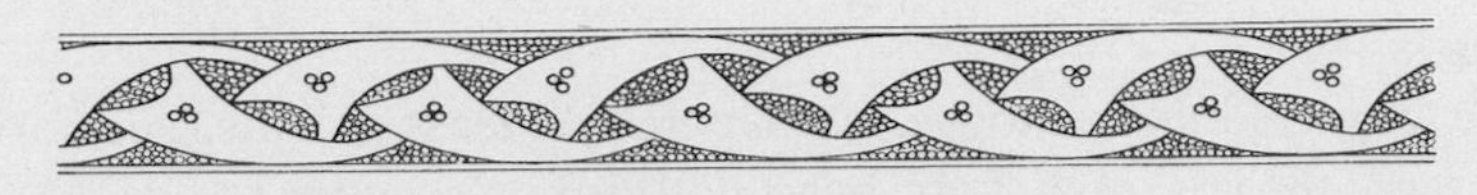

Seeing Feet

Whenever I went down the stairs in our house I looked down to avoid falling. One day my grandmother was watching me.

"Let your feet see for you," she told me. "They'll keep you from falling much better than your eyes! Feel with your toes until you find the edge and let your heels slide down the stair until they find the next one. Put yourself in your center, in the place below your navel, and keep your head high!"

That was fun, and I spent days going up and down the stairs like a queen. This is how I realized, with time, that my feet were "seeing" better and better. I felt my soles become more aware, my feet more sensitive and sensual. I came to trust them more and more, and my balance eventually settled in the lower part of my body.

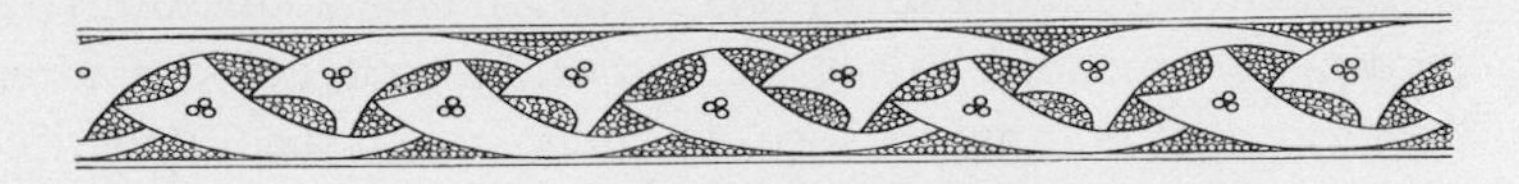

Good Morning, Mystery

Every morning, shortly after sunrise, a Bedouin woman came to our house. Gracefully balanced on her head was the basket full of buffalo cream (*gemar*) that we had for breakfast. Whenever I managed to get up in time, I ran to the front of our house to catch sight of her coming from afar. I was fascinated by the way in which she approached, all dressed in black, quiet and regal, her step steady and confident. I always wondered how it was that the basket never fell and seemed to fit her head like a hat. Once at the house, she removed the basket and greeted me. Together we went inside where my grandmother inspected the cream and decided how much we needed for that day. We drank tea while the Bedouin woman told us the latest news. Then she would get up and replace the basket on her head before leaving. My fascination with the way she carried her basket hadn't escaped my grandmother, yet she did not say a word.

I decided to get to the bottom of this mystery. The next morning, I could hardly wait for the Bedouin woman to arrive. Again, her soft steps carried her down the street.

Before we went into the house, I whispered, "Please, tell me the secret: How can you carry the basket on your head without using your hands?"

She smiled, took the basket down and showed me a round mat made of cloth that I hadn't noticed before.

"Here is the earth, then me, then the mat and then the sky."

"So where is the secret?" I wanted to know.

But she would say no more, so I could only continue to observe her and admire her skill. Only much later would I come to realize the value of what I had witnessed and understand what the secret was really about.

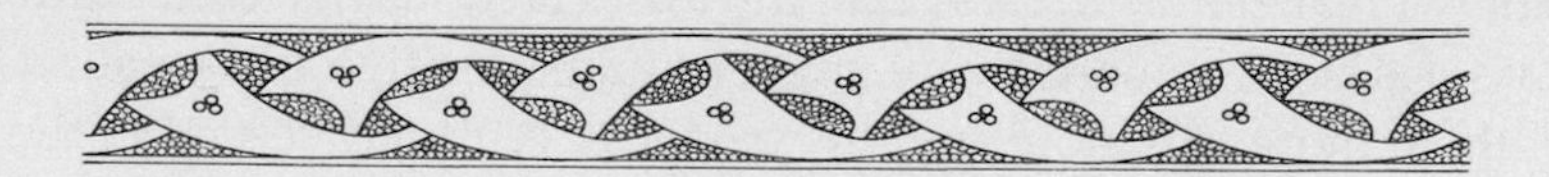

THE TALE OF GIVING AND TAKING

When I was a little girl, I wore my hair long, after an old Bedouin tradition according to which the hair is the seat of the soul. Looking after one's hair was therefore of utmost importance; it was cut only if absolutely necessary.

Every morning, two of my aunts combed my hair. I sat on a stool with one aunt on each side. They parted my hair and together they combed it. The whole episode was usually punctuated by much shouting on my part. Still, they never let it interrupt them and went on combing, unruffled, until my hair was neatly braided in two braids. I was then free to start the day.

Back in the sixties, it was fashionable to weave into one's braids ribbons with two ornate gold drops. In my heart I longed to have some. One day, my grandmother surprised me with this very gift. I was over the moon.

Bursting with pride, I finally wove into my hair the jewels I'd set my heart on. With every step, I could hear them gently jingle around my head and I felt as though I was the most beautiful creature ever to have walked the earth. Nobody could miss my happiness, and all around me rejoiced in it.

Later that day, we were invited to the house of some people I didn't know. The women of our house put on their best clothes and jewelry, draped themseves in their *abayas*, and off we went. I wore my new golden dangles with pride. Upon arriving at our friends' house, we were greeted by a crowd of women and I followed my grandmother nobly into the house.

A somewhat older girl came up to me and exclaimed, "What beautiful golden dangles you have!"

Before I could utter a word, my grandmother turned to me and said, "Take them off and give them to her!"

I couldn't believe what I'd just heard. I should part with those beloved golden dangles, the ones I'd just been given? That could not be! Anger and despair welled up in me, yet I had no choice but to remove the dangles from my hair, and hand them to the stranger. I had to summon all my strength to fight back the tears and keep myself from jumping at my grandmother's throat – or at the girl's. How could my grandmother be so mean, when she knew exactly how much I adored those golden dangles! I spent the rest of the visit in a black hole. While the women, including my grandmother of course, chatted gaily, I sat, silently buried in my sorrows.

On the way home, at long last, my grandmother spoke to me.

"Little Fawzia, only the rich can give, and every gift comes back multiplied."

Opening her hand and extending her fingers, she said, "The giving is the mother of receiving," and closed her fingers into her palm. Although I was somewhat mollified by her words, I still felt empty inside.

Fifteen years later, in Abu Dhabi, I was sitting at the back of an elegant limousine, next to a woman with whom I had been acquainted for only a few hours. She handed me a small leather pouch and said, "This was given to me for you."

Surprised, I took the pouch. When I opened it, I could not believe what my eyes saw. Tears washed down my face as the old familiar golden dangles lay in my palm. They looked just like my memories. Grandmother, O Grandmother, how modest and rich you have made me feel! May God bless me with the heart never to forget that giving is the mother of receiving.

I have kept the golden dangles to this very day and one day, a girl will come and I shall weave them into her hair, so that she may be linked to the long chain of life, the natural cycle of becoming and letting go.

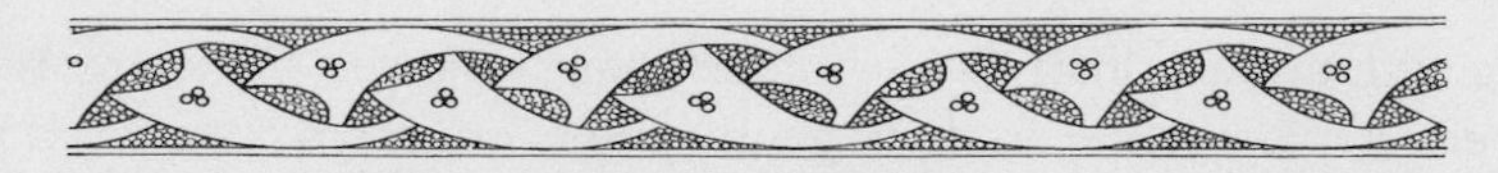

THE MAGIC KITCHEN

There was a room in our house in Baghdad into which no man or child was allowed. This was a holy place for women: the kitchen. My grandmother reigned over her domain like a queen; all the other women did her bidding. When she was not there, I used the opportunity to sneak into this exciting world that was shrouded in mystery.

It was dark in the kitchen; women sat on the floor, all busy. Their scrubbing, cutting, and plucking filled the space. I peered over their shoulders and they smiled at me without interrupting their chores. There was always a huge pot on the stove, steaming away. The air was ripe with the many smells of herbs and spices. Not a single candle, gas lamp or electric bulb in sight. Daylight filtered through an opening high up in the wall. Dimness compelled the women to summon all of their senses for their work. Darkness, damp noises, and the smells rising with the steam, all lent the kitchen an aura of mystery.

At about noon, Amina would sit near the entrance, in semi-darkness. She seemed so frail, as if a gust of wind would knock her over. She was always the first to taste the food, and I was often called to take it to her and feed her.

Flies constantly surrounded Amina; although there were hardly any flies to be seen anywhere else in the house, they sat all over her and buzzed around her incessantly. Amina seemed quite undisturbed and didn't even bother shooing them away. I saw her sitting there for hours with her companions. I always wondered where they came from and why they always stayed with her. When I tried to scare them away, Amina turned her soft, watery eyes to me and said, "Little Fawzia, let them be, they too are God's creatures."

When my grandmother entered the kitchen, nearly swallowed up in the dimness and steam, she checked the women's work and issued various instructions. I would have liked to participate, but every time I asked she drove me away.

"No, not you, not yet," she would say. "It's too dangerous for you!"

This always sounded so serious that I could only obey. Once, I plucked up all my courage and asked why it was that I could not help.

"This is the place where things change shape once their time has come. They take on a different form and fulfill the true purpose of their existence; this is why you are not yet allowed here: your time hasn't come."

Again, I didn't really understand what she meant, but I accepted it and from that time on, I stayed away from the kitchen.

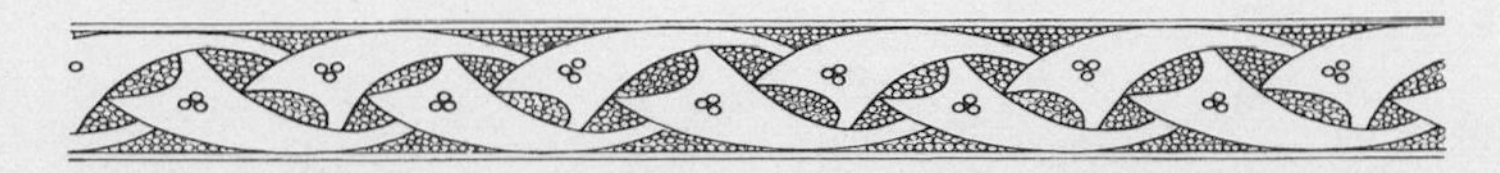

In the Garden of Thoughts

The kitchen's outer wall made part of the garden wall. That was where my grandmother sat. The garden itself was almost square; along the wall grew fruit trees, palm trees, and other trees unknown to me. Surrounded by rosebeds and edged with tiles, grass extended over the center of the garden like a green carpet.

To me, this was my real world, a place that sheltered and nurtured my dreams and fantasies. My longing for infinity grew on this green, between these walls where all greed for material things went quiet. In this garden full of wonders, I was able to discover myself, through play, without any interference from the outside world. It gave me a feeling of utter and all-embracing protection. A sparsely clouded sky covered my garden with its soft blue veil. In one corner grew a giant tree, as tall as my most daring child's thoughts, where several flocks of birds lived twittering and chattering together. The loudest bird was always the cuckoo; to this day, his call takes me right back to my childhood.

My grandmother watched over this garden that had been laid out by my grandfather. Everyday, he came to talk to his roses. He caressed their leaves, his touch infinitely tender and gentle. There was such grief, such longing in his gestures. He told me that whatever the garden gave me, I should pass on. And the garden gave me so much: all the small wonderful creatures that lived there, the bugs and the ants, the birds that flew around and sang, the scorpions that lived beneath the stones and the cats that crept around. They all showed me how true greatness is found in what is small. My sensitivity grew and I became aware of the tiny wishes that become woven into great thoughts.

Behind the walls of our garden lay another garden which belonged to our neighbors, and beyond their walls lay yet another garden. The voices of playing children rose from each of these gardens, which seemed linked in an endless chain. I saw Baghdad as a city of children, a paradise made just for us. Whenever I wanted to see the other children, I'd climb on a ledge, stand on the tip of my toes and peep into the neighbors' garden. To me, this was more exciting than going there, for I could enjoy at one and the same time being alone and having company. What I really loved was being one with all creatures, visible and invisible. My world felt disturbed by outside visitors. And somehow, my intuition told me that this would be but a short, sheltered episode, after which I would soon be set loose into a loud world.

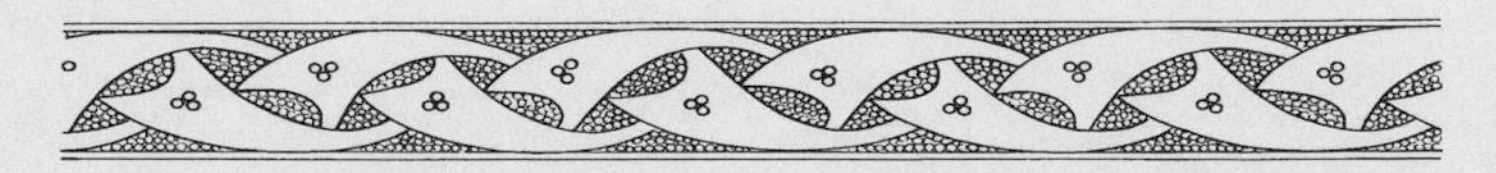

THE OTHER GARDEN

One day, from one of the neighboring gardens, I heard loud shouts that seemed to come out of countless children's mouths. They were so loud and wild that, at first, I just didn't want to know what was going on. But all of a sudden, two pairs of dark eyes looked over the wall into my garden. I felt them instantly and looked back. The eyes belonged to a slightly older boy, maybe seven years old, and to a younger girl. They gestured to me invitingly. I approached cautiously.

"Do you want to play with us? We're playing hopscotch."

"Who's we?" I asked them.

"All of us. Come on!"

All of us—who was "all of us?" I decided to find out—and, in order to avoid any possible confrontation, I didn't ask for permission. So over the wall I climbed, assisted by both children, into the other garden. I was so busy getting myself on top of the wall that I only realized where I was once I found myself in the middle of it.

This garden was indeed different from ours. It was long and didn't quite deserve the name of "garden": except for four huge trees which met at the top and cast shadows over the whole place, nothing grew there. The ground was well-trodden and hard as stone. A seemingly endless swarm of children suddenly stood in front of me and stared.

"Who are you?" I asked, both proudly and fearfully.

The seven-year-old boy in the front replied. "We moved into this empty house a fortnight ago. I'm Ahmad—what's your name?"

"Fawzia." I was about to add half my genealogy but left it at that since he too had only revealed his first name.

The children went back to their game, which involved hopping vigorously in a row of squares engraved on the ground, and then turning around and returning to the starting point. The idea was to jump over the sides of the squares without touching them. I watched for a while. I was barely interested in the game, but the children intrigued me. They were all barefoot and looked really raggedy and neglected. The younger ones had runny noses, which didn't seem to disturb them in the slightest; the older girls, six, maybe seven years old, carried toddlers on their hips and when their turn came to play, they put them on the floor. The toddlers usually cried until someone picked them up again.

"Come on, I'll show you where we live," Ahmad said to me.

Wherever I went, the children would step aside and make way for me, respectfully if not fearfully. I was amazed and I wondered why so many children would shy away from just one child. Still, I was a guest after all and I satisfied myself with that explanation.

We arrived at a mosaic-tiled inner yard surrounded by a two-story house. The air was so thick that it took me a while to catch my breath. It was like being inside a beehive. People poked out of every door, every window, every single gap: women carrying infants and toddlers in their arms or on their hips darted through the yard, hung washing, kneaded dough, washed rice, loudly shouting orders, reprimands, or greetings at each other.

Ahmad looked at me and yelled over the din, "Come over to my mother!"

We crossed the yard to a woman who sat on the floor kneading dough. Middle-aged, Oum Ahmad wore her shoulder-length hair bound in a small headscarf and looked exhausted, but friendly. When she saw us, she jumped to her feet, wiped her hands on her apron and bowed.

"What an honor! Please come sit down!"

Slightly confused, I answered, "The honor is all mine," and took a seat. Ahmad's mother was about to rush inside and demonstrate her hospitality, but I thanked her and begged her to sit down. I wanted to know how many families lived together.

"There's a family in every room, which makes approximately sixty families. We moved in a fortnight ago because we heard that this house was empty and we'll be staying until they throw us out."

My eyes turned to Oum Ahmad's proud belly.

She laughed and said shyly, "I have seven children, praised be Allah! That's plenty, isn't it? I bet your mother doesn't have so many!"

I gave no reply, because I didn't want to hurt her feelings. "No" would mean that my mother could never understand Oum Ahmad's difficult, chore-laden existence and "yes" would not reflect the truth. As I looked around, I saw girls of my age busy with household chores. They fetched wood for the stove, carried massive washing baskets, washed and scrubbed the floor, and seemed really distant from their childhood days. They seemed to relate to their mother as someone with whom they shared both their work and a common destiny; their attitude was brisk yet very intimate.

All of a sudden, there was a big uproar in the garden and one of my grandmother's servants burst in.

"Here you are, Fawzia. We've been looking for you all over the place! Your grandmother's mad at you!"

I stood up at once and made to leave.

"You'll come back, won't you?" asked Oum Ahmad.

"I'll be back," I replied, as the servant shook his head.

I was greeted with severe concern, but that was immaterial. I'd understood something, I'd got to know a new picture, I'd seen an above and a below and discovered a new garden.

A violent discussion ensued between my mother and my grandmother, the first being in favor of my getting closer to and acquainted with this world, the latter all for separation. Yet I wasn't much affected by it all. Whether I went or not didn't matter as much as knowing that Ahmad and Oum Ahmad existed and that there would forever be a place for them in my heart.

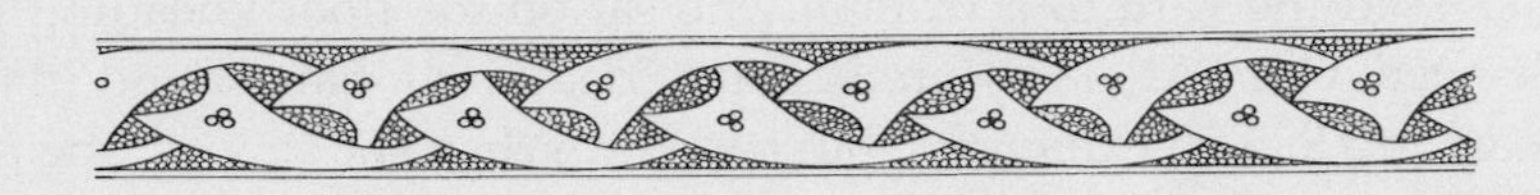

GRANDFATHER, THE QUIET WARRIOR

My grandfather stood a head higher than everyone else, but his real greatness lay in his soul: he was a true warrior, proud, his heart humble and modest. He was our family's protector, its most gifted story-teller, its tireless provider of nourishment and prodigal generosity.

After lunch every day, he lay down for a few hours while the temperature was at its highest. In true Arabic fashion, this afternoon rest lasted from two until five, and it was deemed most inconsiderate to disturb the afternoon peace by visits or anything else.

During the afternoon, the world of fairy tales came alive. We lay down on mattresses on the floor and I sought the dark by putting my head between two mattresses. My grandfather's deep voice carried me into the mythical world of demons, *djinn*, and other wonderful creatures. He told me about proud, powerful women, about their strengths and all the difficulties they encountered and how they always found help through their courage, their faith, and their cunning. Those stories made me into a fighter and gave me the courage to choose and to ask. My grandfather did this in such a light and simple way that it was only much later that I realized the magnitude of his gift.

Because of his unconventional vision of the world, some of my relatives thought of my grandfather as being rather strange. Yet this was precisely what drew me to him.

"Stretch out your hands," he said to me. "Take a good look at them."

I obeyed, eager to discover where he would lead me this time.

"Now imagine your hands turning into a baby's, then into an old woman's, and then again into your hands as they are now."

I held out my hands, one next to the other. I tried to follow his instructions, but nothing happened.

"It's all the same, *Jiddi*," I told him.

"And so it is. There's but a batting of the eyelid between an infant's and an old person's hand, my child." He smiled softly, brought a glass of water to his lips and drank with half-closed eyes. "Whenever you can't understand, little Fawzia, then just wait and let it be. You'll find out that the answer will grow in you, just like desert flowers do. They stay hidden beneath the sand for a long time, and when the rains come, they suddenly sprout and the whole landscape becomes filled with their blossoming pride. Everything grows effortlessly at the right time; one needs only pay attention and listen carefully to recognize this moment. For that you need faith."

In the evenings, when the whole family gathered, my grandfather was the quiet center amid the loud and lively goings on. His usual dish of yoghurt with finely cut cucumber was placed on a low table in front of the sofa where he sat, totally relaxed. I always had the feeling that it was the dish of yoghurt that kept him from disappearing altogether; time and again, he reached for that dish that kept him attached to the material world. My grandfather's quiet, aloof, yet lovingly embracing way gave me the skill of observation. His presence alone sharpened my senses and made me open up so that I could take in as much as possible.

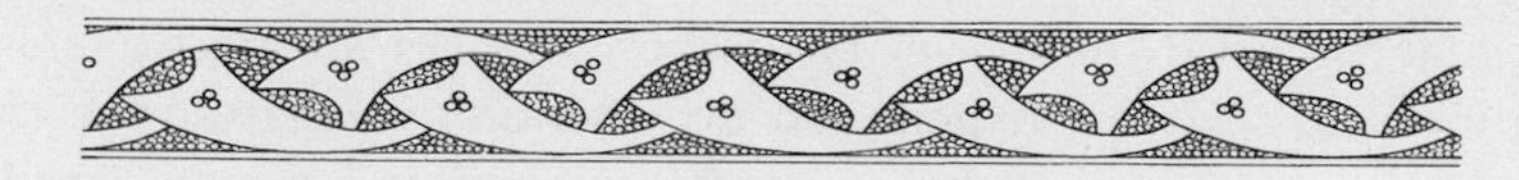

The Dancing Heart

On the first Thursday of every month, our house filled with men who brought with them huge drums, *daffs* (hand-drums), and cymbals. On those days my grandfather donned a long, snow-white *djalabiya* (caftan) and a black, silver-lined *abaya*. He seemed even taller than usual, and radiated dignity and that special balance and harmony that stem from knowing that one is safely cradled in God's hands. Before he joined the other men, he touched the children's heads, leaving behind the heavy scent of amber.

Large, fragrant trays filled with rice, raisins, almonds, pistachio nuts, peas, fried eggs, and morsels of meat, were carried by the young men of the family and their friends into the dining rooms and laid on low, round wooden tables. Steam filled the rooms with the smell of spices and rose water. We all said the afternoon prayers together, and then the men sat together and ate. The women gathered and ate in a separate room.

Toward the end of the afternoon, more women clad in black arrived and joined my grandmother. Tea and small sweet dishes were served.

After sunset prayers, the men gathered in the biggest room in our house. The women had prepared the oil lamplit room, and the fragrance of the best Yemenite incense lingered. Thick upholstered mattresses lay against the walls for the men to sit on. My grandfather sat at one end of the room with the mullah, who began reciting the Koran, praising the Prophet in a deep, loud voice.

Meanwhile the women had sat down in a circle. Their heads were covered with black veils—the color of Mesopotamia, this old between-the-rivers country since the beginning of time. They held their heads slightly bent forward so that the veils slipped over their faces. Among the women was a female mullah who also began praying. Her voice was clear and came from deep in her belly. The women began rocking their trunks back and forth, their bodies moving together in harmony like one huge wave. Just as suddenly as she had started, the mullah fell silent. Each woman sat there, lost in her own meditation. Their veils made them look like beings from another world. Then the drums started beating from the men's room; the heavy, overpowering rhythm flowed over us and swept the women away. They bowed, slowly at first, starting with the right, then to the front, raising their heads in the middle to bend them again to the left... *la ilaha illa llah... la ilaha illa llah...* (There is no god but God). Devotion filled their voices and the room vibrated in harmony. Grandmother sat outside the circle and moved the prayer beads between her strong fingers while murmuring softly. My excitement and my attention went from the circle of women to my grandmother who, as usual, remained in her own world.

Because of my young age, I still enjoyed the privilege of being exempted from the separation of the sexes. I was allowed to move freely between the women's and the men's room. I stole into the latter and observed the dancers' wild movements, the sweat running down the drummers, and my grandfather's all-embracing personality, before creeping back to the women. However different they were, in some way I didn't quite understand, these two worlds seemed to complete each other. The fragrance of incense mixed with the smell of the women's bodies. The movements became always wilder, forward and backward, forward and backward, until they melted into one wild toing and froing of heads. Some women started sobbing. The older women seemed more collected and calmed the younger ones by hugging them and holding their hands, before collapsing.

Their shoulders were limp, their hair loose. They seemed exhausted, out of themselves, yet unable to stop. The beat of the drums quieted, becoming softer and softer. I never knew whether this ritual went on for minutes or for hours. It was as if time and space could no longer be perceived through human senses. The women sat in a circle, their faces reddened and their eyes sparkling. They seemed relieved, happy, and collected. Slowly the ritual came to an end and they leaned against the wall. Someone came in with a tray of dark, sweet tea. Each of them drank silently, wiped the sweat from her face with her veil and, slowly, daily reality came back. Normal conversations started, women kissed and hugged, while the room was filled with incredible softness.

Grandmother ended the ritual with a prayer: "For all beings, visible and invisible, for all minerals, plants and animals, for all people, present and distant. A prayer for all children, for all sick and suffering people, for all searchers and loners, for all masters, male and female, who have come and will come, and for all the prophets..."

She then said the prayer for all, while those in attendance stretched their open hands to heaven before bringing them down and stroking their faces and their bodies. Fruit, nuts and dried fruit were then served and, at the end, small cups of strong, dark coffee with much cardamom. One after the other, the guests took their leave. A special day had drawn to a close.

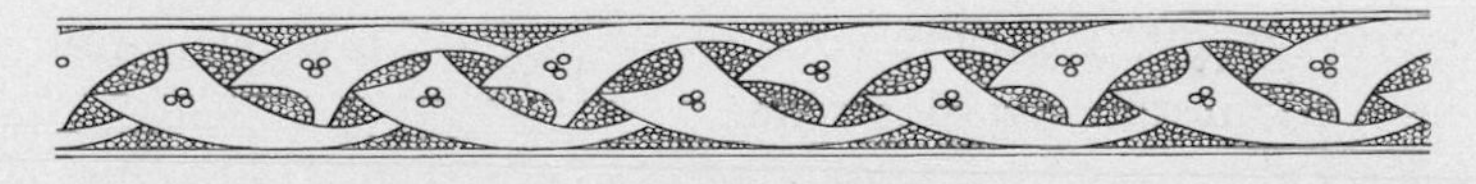

Oh, the Ball!

"Grandmother, where are we going?" We sat in the back of a black taxi and the ride had been long.

"To distant relatives of mine. You'll like it there, you'll see."

We arrived at a big villa. My grandmother knocked loudly on a wooden door, half of which was hidden behind a huge bush. After a while, the door opened and a woman appeared, with amazingly long, blond hair and large, sad eyes. I could but gape. Never in my life had I seen a blond woman. Was she human or did she come from another world?

The blonde lady was clearly pleased and at the same time surprised by our visit. We followed her into the house, where we were greeted by a peculiar smell.

"I'm making jam," said the blonde creature. "It's nearly ready."

"Grandmother, what's jam?" My grandmother laughed. She turned to the blonde lady who was supposed to be our relative.

"Little Fawzia doesn't know jam—we don't make any at home."

Then she looked at me and explained how to make jam by cooking fruit and sugar into a thick syrup. "You can eat it with bread," she told me.

I looked at this strange, blonde creature uncomprehendingly. Why is this woman cooking valuable, good fruit into a weird sauce, I thought to myself. This only reinforced my feeling that she must come from some other world. Also, the house was huge and no one else seemed to be living in it. I didn't feel comfortable and discreetly pushed my grandmother to go, but she paid no heed. Both women talked about a variety of matters and people. However hard I tried to concentrate, I only understood scraps of conversation: "... reinforce the families ... still so young ... make a quick decision..."

Once more, my grandmother was talking in riddles. She always did that when she wanted no one to understand except the person she spoke to directly. She turned her body so that she faced the person fully and only moved her lips ever so slightly.

Suddenly the door opened and in came the most handsome boy I had ever laid eyes on. He was tall, slim as a cypress tree, his complexion neither light nor dark, with thick, dark hair that framed his clear forehead and an intensity that made his dark eyes glow. He came closer, bowed to the blond creature, took and kissed her hand and said, "*As-salamu alaykum*, peace be with you, mother!"

... Mother! This blond creature was his mother? How could that be? I was totally beside myself. Then the young boy greeted my grandmother, who hugged him and introduced him to me.

"This is Scha'ban, a young man of good manners and noble descent."

"So I see," I answered politely, averting my face from his glowing eyes.

"Show Fawzia the garden," said the blond mother.

I stood up wordlessly and we went into the garden. We stood there next to each other and although I didn't know what was going on, I felt that it had something to do with this beautiful, quiet boy. So, I thought to myself, I shall try and find out as much as I can about him.

"How old are you, Scha'ban?"

"I'll be eleven in a couple of months."

"You live here alone with your mother, don't you?"

"Yes, my parents are divorced and the time has come for me to go to my father's. But my mother cannot let go of me."

That's why the sad eyes, I thought. Poor blond woman. Now I even understood why she would cook fresh fruit.

Suddenly, I began to understand even more. My grandmother wanted to help the woman and she wanted to do so by marrying us children. In this way she would kill two birds with one stone. Through our marriage Scha'ban would not be lost to his mother, and I would get a bridegroom of noble descent, besides which he came from my grandmother's side of the family, which meant she would hold the reins.

Fine, grandmother, I thought, but first I must see whether I also agree and whether this young boy matches my wishes. I saw a ball and turned to Scha'ban.

"What a beautiful ball!"

Without a word, he went to pick it up and brought it to me. I kept throwing it up in the air, as we wandered slowly around the garden. When we came to a tall tree, I threw it in such a way that it was caught in the branches.

"Oh!" I cried, "the ball!"

Scha'ban looked up and then he looked at me; I smiled. Again, he acted quickly and without many words. He fetched a ladder, leaned it against the tree, climbed up the ladder and then up the strong branches. He reached the ball and only gave it to me once he was down. He was well educated and generous. I had found out everything that I needed to know. My grandmother was already calling for us to leave. I gave Scha'ban one more look and I ran off.

Once in the car, we sat quietly next to one another. Grandmother's direct question broke the silence.

"Can you see yourself marrying Scha'ban?"

"Yes," I replied, although, to be perfectly honest, I wasn't quite sure what "marrying" meant.

"Your mother will be against it," muttered my grandmother, lost in her own thoughts.

And so it was. My mother tore her hair at the thought of marrying off her six-year old daughter.

"They will only be promised to each other," my grandmother pleaded, "and they will marry only later."

"Why the rush?"

"He comes from one of this country's best families and has all the qualities one can wish for in a man."

It came to a great tug-of-war between the two women, which nevertheless left me rather indifferent.

Today, I am grateful that my mother came out victorious. I never saw Scha'ban again, although to this day, whenever he and his blond mother cross my memories, I find myself drifting away in thoughts. Was he strong enough to stay near his vulnerable mother? Who did he marry? Did he develop his noble character and become a wise and sensitive man?

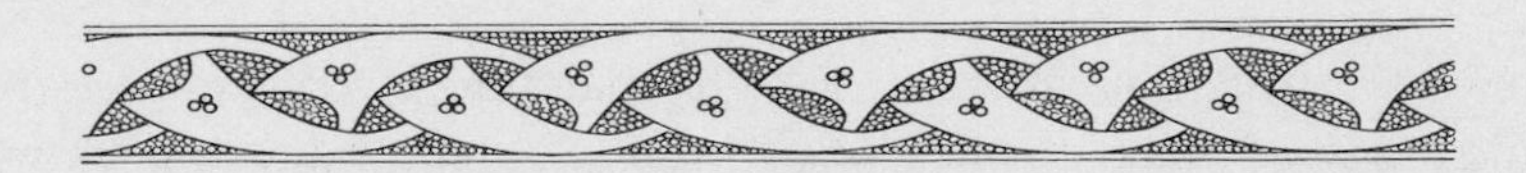

A WOMEN'S WORLD

Ever since I turned four, my grandmother had been taking me along whenever she paid her visits. She always dressed very modestly; unlike other women I observed, she cared neither for jewels nor for magnificence. When we left the house, she put on her black *abaya*, which covered her from head to toe. In Baghdad, all the older women donned such *abayas* when they left their homes. Since they all looked the same, colored threads on the lower hem helped distinguish them from one another. My grandmother had a red thread in the shape of five little crosses. I was always very impressed by this *abaya* because it made her look solemn, unapproachable and seemed to be the symbol of a secret sisterhood.

Our visits usually took us to large gatherings, to which women of all ages came with their children. Friends who were particularly close to the hostess helped her serve and clear up. When a meal was planned, they helped with the preparations, and they could also count on being helped when they were the hostesses.

The women chatted, drank tea, ate Arabic sweets, exchanged news, and discussed their worries and problems. The activities, reactions and feelings of each woman were shared and commented on. There seemed to be no end to the giving and receiving of mutual criticism and praise, well-intentioned advice, and comments born from experience. There was openness and trust between the women. A deep honesty permeated those meetings and created a feeling of well-being, which put aside all reverence and ladylike attitudes. One woman opened her legs shamelessly when she felt in the mood to talk, another flung herself to the floor in laughter. The naked truth was told without any window-dressing, weak spots were tickled, silly things said and done and laughter came from deep in the belly, so that these gatherings made the women stronger, giving them the courage to see things in a different light and take them with a lighter heart.

Of course, the women also talked about the lives and attitudes of the men, their jobs, their high or low income and their striving to improve the family's social position. Their behavior within the family was discussed quite openly, right down to their sex lives. Women often made fun of their own desires, their own sexuality and overpowering sensuality, in such an obvious way that, although we girls couldn't quite understand it all, we shared in their laughs while at the same time receiving a social and sexual education.

Excitement always reached its peak when one of women got up to turn on music, tie a scarf around her hips, and slowly sway into another world, dancing for us. All the attention focused on her, tension grew in the bodies of the other women. They stood up, their eyes filling with an old, so far forgotten knowledge as they began to spur on the dancer—

"How beauiful is the shape of her eyes, blessed be Allah!"

"Brave and strong as bamboo stem!"

"Hold your head high, proud Fatima!"

"She dyes her hair with henna!"

"Have you seen how pampered her feet are?"

"Look how softly her hips are circling!"

The onlookers clapped in rhythm and trilled shrilly, conveying their enthusiasm.

"Ya ayni, ya ayni!" (Oh you, light of my eyes!)

"Ya leli, ya leli!" (Oh you, darkness of my night!)

The acclamations were wild and our excitement made us talk all at the same time. Joy exploded in shouts. The women experienced all their beauty and all their feminity in a relaxed and supportive atmosphere. Once the dancer finished, she took her scarf and tied it around another woman's hips, thereby passing the dance over. Often two women danced together, completing and inspiring each other. I loved it when life was in effervescence like that, when we were among ourselves.

Whenever a little girl ran to the dancers in the middle of the room and started dancing, the faces of the older women lit up, they laughed loudly, for life had taken on a new rhythm, a rhythm that was before us and would continue after we had gone. Of course, these performances were also used by the mothers-in-law to take a close look at their future daughters-in-law. And we girls knew about it! Yet when an old woman got up to dance, suddenly, something was there that could not be expressed in words—a gift, a woman's prayer filled the room, borne by the subtle, nearly wise movements of one who stood far ahead of us in the long chain of women. So when an old woman got up to dance and show her mature sensuality and her old beauty, we kissed her hands gratefully while smiling at her cheekily.

My grandmother took me to many such gatherings and every time I watched, fascinated, and listened closely to the older women. They gave each other advice about their appearance and their behavior and enjoyed their beauty. Since they could laugh about their weaknesses, they shared them without shame or fear. Never were any nasty comments to be heard, "You're too fat" or "You're too thin," "Your breasts are too big" or "Your breasts are too small." Each body shape was seen as a gift, an intended destiny.

It was a duty to make the best out of it. If some were pretty and others less so, well *nasib,* "Destiny!" Compassion towards oneself and others was part of their philosophy of life.

Even women who didn't particularly like each other never failed to behave politely and respectfully. The Arabic language itself, with all its greetings and polite forms, did not allow them to be rude to each other. There was nevertheless gossip, but this too was part of being a woman. The community found itself enriched by the existence of every single woman. As girls, we received all of this through these gatherings, through *our* women's rituals. So we were helped on our way to womanhood, motherhood, and old age.

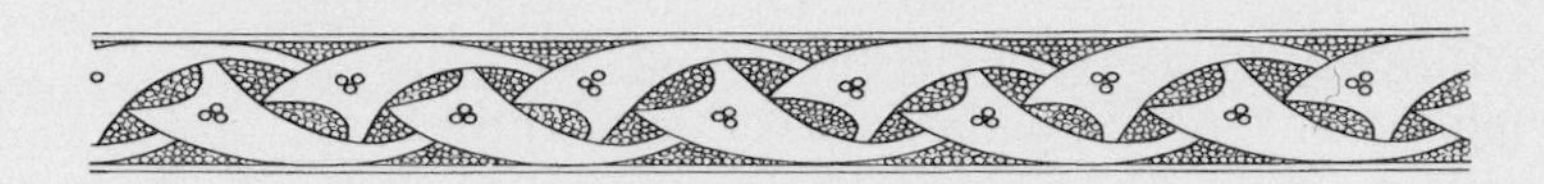

BLOOD FLOWS

I knew this day would come and change my whole life; my mother had told me about it often enough. But not just now! Fear overcame me and I felt the world darken around me. I ran to my room and thought about what I could do. Could I maybe keep it a secret? Pretend nothing had happened? I thought for a long time and then I decided to go to my mother.

"Mother, she's arrived," I said quietly and with a sad expression.

My mother looked at me and her whole face lit up. She came closer and plunged her eyes into mine.

"Congratulations, my daughter. You've become a woman!" I couldn't understand why she was happy, when my whole world was falling apart. Mother hugged me and before I could say a word, the whole family knew about the "happy" news. All the women came and smiled at me. I was now one of them.

"Today we'll cook your favorite dish," said one of them.

Another brought me a shawl as a gift. My aunt gave me a colorful piece of material, and promised she would make me a particularly beautiful dress. All of a sudden, several towels appeared, which were extended to me with laughs. I found the whole thing extremely uncomfortable and would have preferred to remain by myself. But I knew this was not acceptable. Now I had to let the others' exuberance delight over me.

Mother came into my room with a little box, pressed it in my hand and asked me to open it. Curious, I opened the box and beheld a ring set with a pearl.

"I had this ring specially made for this occasion," she said. I smiled weakly as she put the ring on my finger. Thanks came through my lips with great effort. The ring was a symbol for my newly-acquired status as a prisoner. At any rate, this is how I felt about it at the time. Then all the women present sat with me in a circle.

My mother started speaking gently. "Now my daughter, you've become a woman and this means that you should also behave like one. Your duties and your behavior are now going to change, my little one."

I knew what was about to happen, for I had already noticed before how after this event girls disappeared from the children's group and stopped belonging to us.

"You know," my mother went on, "it is no longer acceptable for you to play in the streets with the boys. Now you are different and you will remain among your own kind."

Tears welled in my eyes. I didn't want to become different, I didn't want to give up my games and my freedom to go where I pleased.

"Suitors will soon start knocking on our door," said our cook, laughing.

"And all the mothers-in-law will be watching you," my aunt added.

"Now you too can have an *abaya* like your grandmother, if you like," my other aunt said encouragingly. But even that gift didn't seem to help.

"Couldn't we wait a little longer, Mother?" I asked shyly. I wanted at least to say goodbye to my playing companions.

"But that can't be!" my aunt replied. "The blood is flowing and everything must take its course."

So there was no running away. With a heavy heart, I accepted my entry into the women's world. I looked at them, these round, full beings with their swinging movements and I just couldn't see myself being like them. Deep in my heart, I decided to retain everything childish. The fire of rebellion, which was to be my companion for many years to come, rose in me.

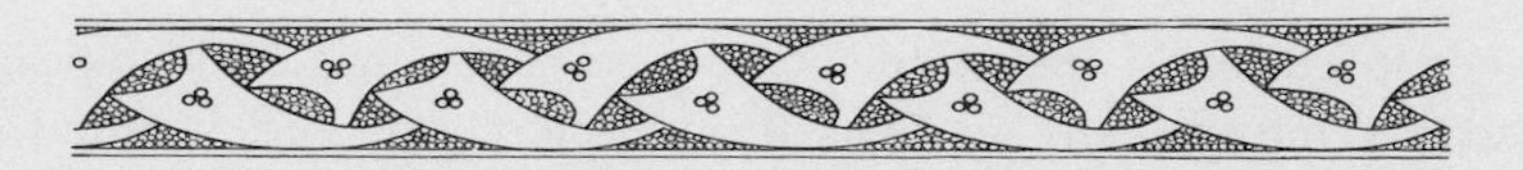

THE GREAT CELEBRATION

One day, the women in my family decided there would be a celebration in our house. The preparations took three whole days. I helped tirelessly. Everyone was excited and the whole house was filled with the industrious activities of the women.

When the big day arrived, as the guests filled the room and the air thickened, Aunt Lahib, my father's sister, called me and said, "So Fawzia, now your time has come. You'll be allowed to dance in front of our guests for the first time!"

This nearly knocked the breath out of me. My knees started trembling. My eyes were opened suddenly and I realized the meaning of this celebration. Given a chance, I'd have run away, but my aunt stood in front of me, so powerful, with her smile so bright. Though that smile seemed more like a snarl to me, I couldn't escape. Yet at the same time the sweet smell of fight mixed with my fear and pushed me to take up the challenge. I would not enter this room as a victim, I would enter as Fawzia!

And so it was.

My aunt gave me a scarf, which I tied around my hips. I listened to the music for an instant, and in I walked. All the guests turned to me and smiled encouragingly. I started moving slowly, getting in harmony with the rhythm. I felt stiff and clumsy. I suffered from all the concentrated attention.

Then my eyes fell upon my grandmother. She was sitting quietly among the guests and her eyes stroked me briefly. Her calm gave me confidence and I glided deeper into the circling movements. Slowly, the audience disappeared and soon I didn't even notice my grandmother any longer. I heard my heartbeat give me the rhythm and I felt my body dissolve in movements much older than me. Happiness and pride overwhelmed me and a deep inner knowledge curled my lips into a smile. I don't know how long I danced, because my sense of time had melted into the heat of my dancing. The inner and the outer worlds were touching. At that moment, I was neither young nor old. Eternity beckoned inside me and I gave in to the call of Life and danced with the intensity and fervor of Life itself. When I stopped and ran out of the room, I heard the guests clap and I knew that I had completed my initiation successfully. I was nine years old: a woman and a child at the same time.

After this dance, my grandmother stopped giving me orders and the word "little" was no longer used in front of my name. My dancing had carried me into a new world. Now I had the right to choose myself how I wanted to go on in it.

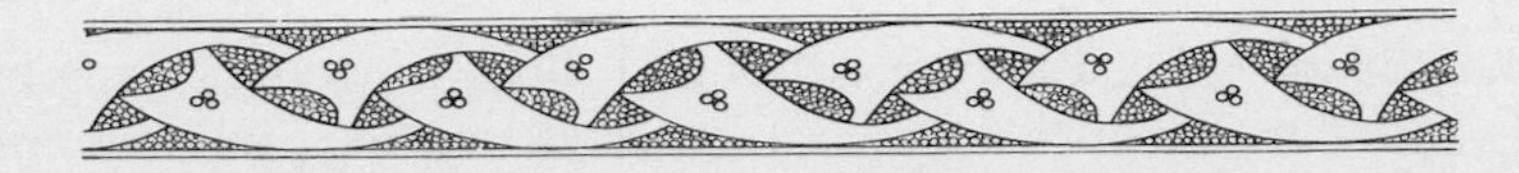

MY NEW WORLD

My journey to Europe began. The instability of the political situation tore my family away from Baghdad and took us to Lebanon; yet trouble and wars boiled there, too, and I was taken even further away from my cradle, that land-between-two-rivers, Mesopotamia.

Now when I look back on my childhood, I realize that the outer world, namely the world outside the family circle, was always full of trouble, suppressed revolts, and flaring wars which left deep marks in the protected family circle. Doors flung open, breathless messengers rushed in, and silent, remote family councils were held, in which people spoke only in whispers, with heavy heads bent forward, and silent, salty tears flowing down brave women's faces.

As children, we learned to bear the strokes of fate with dignity and not to drown in the whirling and blows of the moment. Shouting, flaring tempers, crying, and other eruptions were indeed allowed, but they were to be experienced as a deeper breath, while the "true essence" of a human being flowed on gently in the fate ascribed by God. To strengthen this attitude and keep a clear sight, the older members of the family would tell us stories about our ancestors. And the ancestral chain was long and went all the way to our Beloved Prophet, the greatest of all our models. The world, *ad-dounya,* was made of the strangest things and events, the elders told us; it had valleys and mountains, ponds and wild rivers and, come what may, it was our duty never to forget the essential: namely, that we were both servants and masters of a greater power.

I had insisted on completing my school education. At the time, we were living in Lebanon, where the schools had been closed for several months because of the spreading civil war. Since I couldn't go to school there, my family decided to send me to relatives in Europe. I would go alone, since my family hoped that the situation would cool down within a couple of months and I could then return.

My destiny was to be different. I spent my first days in Europe crying, sitting near a stove. It was so cold. Everything was so foreign to me. I just couldn't see how I would live in this world. Yet my curiosity was greater than the pain I felt at the loss of my home and childhood world. I observed my new world carefully and what struck me most were the women. They were so different from those I was used to at home. They seemed more like men. In turn, the men seemed much softer than the ones I had known at home. I saw women with long hair on their legs and short hair on their heads; I saw them wearing pants and hurrying through the streets with long strides.

In this world, everything was nice and tidy, and disciplined reason was the system unto which all were gathered.

People darted through the streets, following an invisible goal, everyone busy with oneself. The whole world was made of tiny human islands, each drifting solitary in the ocean. Laughing was felt as obscene and loud talking did not exist. Nothing was allowed to disturb the peace and quiet. Yet they were all very polite to one another. Everyone seemed to leave you in peace without interfering, as long as you abided by the almighty rule of order. Did that mean that I too could do as I pleased? Youngsters kissed in public and nothing happened, apart from the occasional member of the older generation shaking head. Young men and women walked together in the streets, quite relaxed, chatting and touching each other, without seeming to think twice about it. This new world was interesting, because the limitations of my old world no longer existed. Yet something appeared to be missing; something essential escaped me. I was in danger of losing my bearings. I was afraid that the meaning of things would escape me.

Many years passed during which I lived in this new world, watching the people around me, living with them and trying to understand their way of life. Losing myself in the flow of this new life, not knowing where I belonged, I needed a form in which I could express my inner thoughts, tensions, and feelings. I longed for a way to bring my inner and outer world into a dialogue.

Part Two: A History of Women's Dancing

Thoughts toward the furthering of the dance of the feminine belly and pelvis, or an attempt to complete the history of the awareness of the feminine body...

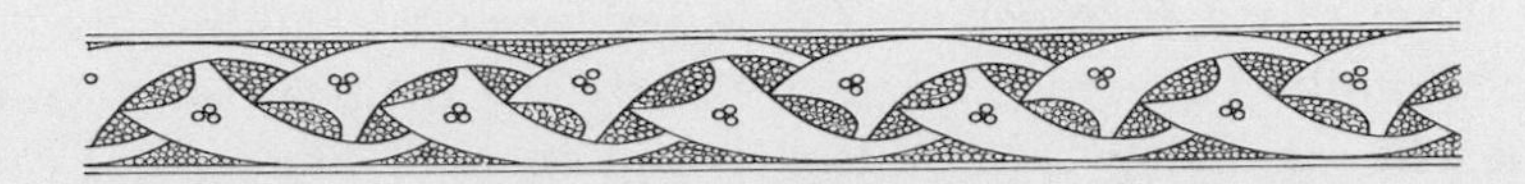

Primitive Peoples and Dancing

In this context, "primitive" does not refer to any historical period, defined in terms of time and space, but rather to an inner level of awareness. Primitive peoples saw themselves as incarnations of the Great Mother's children; to them, there was no separation between the body and the world, inside and outside, this life and the next: all things were indissolubly united. The "self" was as yet undeveloped; a matriarchal holistic vision reigned. This harmonious relationship to the world can be traced through early symbols, which in turn gave birth to myths and rituals.

Originally, all rituals were danced; body and mind were set in motion as a unity. Through dancing, primitive peoples expressed their natural excitement and deep emotions.

Rituals and their particular dances strengthened the bonds between members of the community, expressed joy and pleasure, or praised life; but also it was through these dances that men and women tried to understand the mystery of life, nature—and above all, birth and death, the greatest mysteries of all. Rituals were therefore used as incantations to further growth on earth, to help the clouds break into rain, or to celebrate acts of fertility.

In matriarchal horticultural and agricultural societies, women secured most of the basics for survival and held key social positions. It was also through women that the ecstatic dances were made into major social events.[1]

A major characteristic of all matriarchal cults was dancing. Dance was more than a passing emotional outburst, beyond even expressive prayer: indeed, dancing was the most important magical practice of all. Dancing is the oldest and most elementary form of spiritual expression; it is magic in the form of a danced ritual. All the other modes of expression that we have come to know by the name of Art have developed from dancing.[2]

It is because of their magical bond to the living and their knowledge of the mysteries of life that women became guides, and later priestesses who served the feminine goddesses. Through the seemingly endless succession of mothers and daughters, women became the mortal representatives of the Great Mother Earth, and the movements of their dancing reflected this. As the bearer of life, a woman was most strongly connected to her body and its changes, as well as to the pulse of life itself. In the Sahara, a cave painting from the Stone Age illustrates well her special status. It represents a hunting man and a woman with her arms raised, their genitals connected by a line. This line, itself a sort of magical umbilical cord, expresses clearly the magical function of the feminine. She was the giver of protection and strength. She had the capacity to connect to higher forces and preserve the unity of people, nature, and the world of plants and animals. This connection to nature and the body awareness that ensued manifested themselves through dancing.

One can assume that women had their own understanding of the changes in their bodies. They knew exactly when they ovulated and recognized the accompanying external signs just before and after; they observed the swelling and falling of the breast when the blood flowed and the special sensitivity, close to clairvoyance, that accompanied this cycle and strengthened their visionary powers. They recognized the changes at the time of conception and they may have known the dreams that announced a pregnancy. In this, they were helped by living in nature and feeling connected to it.

This is how a woman partook in the pulse of life, which she revered more intensely than a man ever could. Both man and woman acknowledged the inner laws of human life and nature, and this was reflected in their belief in the Great Mother, the Great Feminine.

One of the oldest archetypes of the Great Mother was Ashar, better known as Ishtar. This Babylonian goddess symbolized, on the one hand, the earth and fertility; on the other hand, death and destruction. She was often represented with burning eyes, the symbol of light and spirit, and a burning navel, the symbol of fertility and death.

In these representations, the earth, which is taken as feminine reality, is the body, and its center is the navel, from which the world receives its nourishment. A moon crescent crowned Ishtar's head. Like Demeter, Ishtar is often shown with ears of corn sprouting from her shoulders, rooting her firmly to the earth and its fruit.

In a culture in which fertility was a matter of survival, the connection between sexuality, menstruation, and birth was part of everyday knowledge. And it was obvious that the moon played a part in it all. The moon cycle, with its waxing and waning, came to symbolize the eternal cycle of conception and birth (a small crescent on the horizon), growth (from the first quarter to the full moon), decay and dying (a waning moon), death (the three moonless nights at new moon), and rebirth (when the tiny crescent reappears).[3] It therefore made sense that the goddess of fertility be the moon goddess. She came to rule over the life-giving element of water: the seas and the oceans as well as the brooks and the rivers. She became, purely and simply, the origin of the feminine: the Great Goddess. During her light phases, she dispensed life and fertility; during her dark phases she wreaked nature's death and destruction. In most cultures, there were several moon goddesses, at least one for each phase. The Great Goddess was known under many names, of which these are but a few:

In the Middle East: Inanna, Ishtar, Tiamat, Astarte
In Egypt: Isis, Hathor, Neith, Maat
In Greece: Demeter, Hera, Artemis, Aphrodite, Persephone, Hecate, Europa
In ancient Rome: Juno, Diana, Luna, Titania
In the Far East: Shakti, Aditi, Durga (India), Tara (Tibet), Kwan Yin (China), Kannon (Japan).[4]

The following, well-known myth retraces primitive peoples' explanation for the change of seasons, as well as their winter worry that the earth would never be fertile again. This particular version tells us about Ishtar; it dates approximately 4,500 BC.

> *When Ishtar's husband, Tammouz, died* (to this very day *Tammouz* means July in Arabic) *and returned to the world of darkness, the womb of the earth, Ishtar decided to save him by craft and to bring back the light. She dressed up in all her splendor, tied a girdle around her hips and donned seven veils to enter the netherworld through seven gates. The goddess of love danced seductively at each gate, each time leaving one veil to gain entrance. At the seventh gate, she removed the last veil. During the whole of her stay in the underworld, all life on earth stood still, deprived of love, growth, and celebration. Only when Ishtar returned, fully veiled to shield her secret from human eyes, did life on earth blossom again. Her reunion with Tammouz was celebrated every year at the beginning of spring and symbolized the reawakening of nature and life.*[5]

Ishtar's dance of the veils survived throughout history. It was given several interpretations according to different social attitudes toward women.

Although we can only guess at Ishtar's seduction dance, it seems reasonable to assume that her movements must have resembled those of belly dancing. The girdle or scarf still tied around the hips by every Middle Eastern dancing woman reminds us of Ishtar's dance and transforms today's woman into an interpreter of a culture long gone.

Nearly all myths about human history contain similar stories of death and rebirth in the natural world; time and again, they are experienced through dancing.

In matriarchal times, the moon played a major role. Priority was given to the night in matriarchal consciousness. Day and light are born from night and darkness, and not the other way round. This perception has been kept in the Arabic language, in which the day begins on the previous night. If your birthday were on, say, March 15th, in the Arab world you would begin celebrating the evening of the 14th. You begin counting the day at sunset, rather than sunrise. And to this day, the yearly and monthly calendars revolve around the moon cycle.

Since the beginning of humankind, the inhabitants of the earth have observed the sky and tried to measure time on the basis of the celestial bodies. The phases of the moon were easy to recognize. The first time unit, after day and night, is therefore likely to have been the lunar month. In prehistoric times, the moon cycle was already written, or rather engraved, on bones or stones. Archeologists have found such lunar calendars going back to time between 40,000 and 8,000 BC: one small stroke for a normal sun day, a longer stroke for a full or a new moon. Some cave drawings nearly that ancient, such as those discovered in Spain, are even more precise: in the middle is a human-like lunar goddess, surrounded by waxing and waning moon crescents, one thin stroke for the new moon, three dots for the full moon and the following day.[6] The concept of a month had thus been defined: there are 29 days and nights from one full or new moon to the next. Twelve lunar months make a lunar year. And man made further realizations: even during hot summer nights, at the time of the full moon, the fields are covered with dew, the human skin is more intensely irrigated, and more children are born. The feminine cycle was known to be ruled by the moon; menstruation calendars can be found that go back as far as 30,000 BC. These calenders marked auspicious times for conception, as well as the number of lunar months until the expected time of birth.

Since the influence of the moon on the feminine cycle was so well-known, it came as no surprise that women gathered for rituals once a month. These blood and fertility rituals happened mostly during the night, to the exclusion of men. The places chosen for such rituals were usually hills or other elevated places. The hills symbolize the feminine, as they rise gently above the earth, like the belly.

And it was on top of the hill, on the navel of the earth, that the women of these primitive societies danced. (It is interesting to note that, to this day, most holy places on this earth are atop hills; albeit on an unconscious level, the feminine earth symbolism can still be traced). These dances revolved around fertility and therefore the belly played a major part. The dances were used to strengthen sexual energy, to awaken joy, and to praise the mysteries of life. The women danced their dance, a dance that corresponded to their body and expressed all the moods and feelings, all the longings, sufferings, and joys of being a woman. Through their dance, they came into harmony with the universe, abandoning themselves to life and to the divine. What dance could express this more clearly and passionately than belly dance? It can indeed be considered the oldest dance ever danced by a woman, purely and simply the oldest dance in the whole of civilization.

Dancing expressed the longing to stretch beyond one's limitations and come closer to the divine. Prayer was all-embracing in those days; people did not set any limitations on emotions or feelings as they prayed. The whole body shook with worship, and dance helped them open themselves completely. People used their bodies as tools to reach a spiritual level. Their bodies gave them the opportunity to dissolve the self and come closer to the divine. To this day, this technique is used in many religions. For instance, the mystics of Islam, the Sufis, use century-old movements and dances to reach a state in which they recall the divine original. These sacred dances are called *dhikr*, which means calling or re-calling God. The Arabic word for dance, *raqs*, also means "to make the heart quiver and shake."

The drum originally accompanied all these sacred dances. Its beat was the heart's. The inner rhythm of the heart dissolved all sense of time and space. The dancers lingered in the intense experience of the moment. Past and future swung in the moment of being and all mortal pain vanished in the knowledge of the essence.

The first temples built to honor the divine were dedicated to goddesses and served by priestesses. The priestesses danced for the goddess and united with her through their dancing. The energy that was thus released in their bodies was passed on to the temple's visitors, who fed at this divine force. This is how the cult dance became a temple dance.

The strongest energy that can be formed in the body is sexual energy. The movements that arouse that energy most intensely are the circling, bouncing, and vibrating motions of the hips and the pelvis, as well as the contractions of the belly—all part of belly dancing.

The old feminine lunar religions declined in about 3,000 BC. In many cultures, matriarchy was replaced by patriarchy. The moon goddesses were

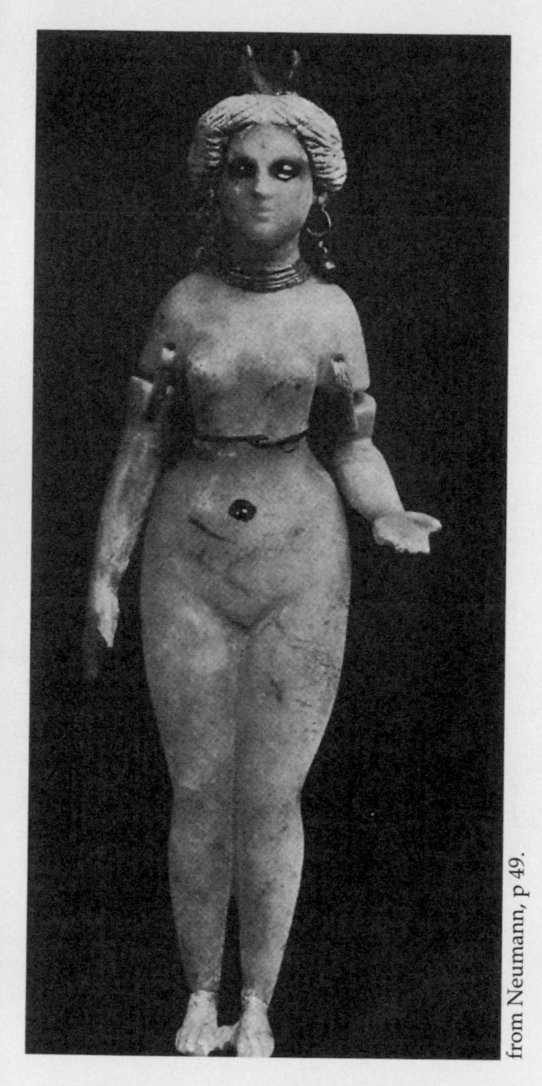

from Neumann, p 49.

Ishtar: Goddess of Life and Death

relegated completely to the zone of darkness and magic. The era of solar mythology started and with it came the domination of male consciousness. The older, matriarchal conception of the world was replaced by a hierarchical-patriarchal worldview and the feminine was no longer acknowledged and respected in its multiple faces. Darkness (or the new moon) was henceforth seen as negative, even though it reflects only one aspect of the lunar principle and feminine origin.

Early people understood that the strength of new life comes from the dark phase of the moon. As the centuries went by, they were to forget this truth and begin to fear the dark side of the moon. This view was given strong support in the subsequent era of solar divinities and can still be seen today.[7]

The partnership and complementarity of man and woman became distorted, as the feminine connection to nature and life, as well as woman's proud strength, came to be considered dark, profane, and dangerous for man's "spiritual" efforts. Yet man remained fascinated and attracted by this force; like a red thread, this dilemma extends throughout male history into contemporary times. Every culture and religion attempted to solve this "problem" in its own way.

The transition from lunar to solar mythology did not occur spontaneously, but fluidly. Many rituals of the Great Mother survived after the decline of the holistic matriarchal conception of the world and many a symbol was adopted and given new interpretations in the male myths.

As the times changed, so did women's dance. It took on a different sense and a new meaning. The sensuality and earth-connected sexuality expressed by women through their dance, their seduction into life, no longer served women and the mystery of being, but instead served to entertain and stimulate the onlookers.

Originally, the sacred women's dance, in which the movements of the hips and pelvis were dominant, was present all around the world. In those times, dancing was still a form of prayer and worship, and religion an integral part of everyday life. Yet with the development of primitive cultures into many layers, the new beliefs repressed the rituals that belonged to the old beliefs. This is how women's belly dance died in many parts of the world. Yet in some places the sacred dancing ritual developed into an entertainment dance.

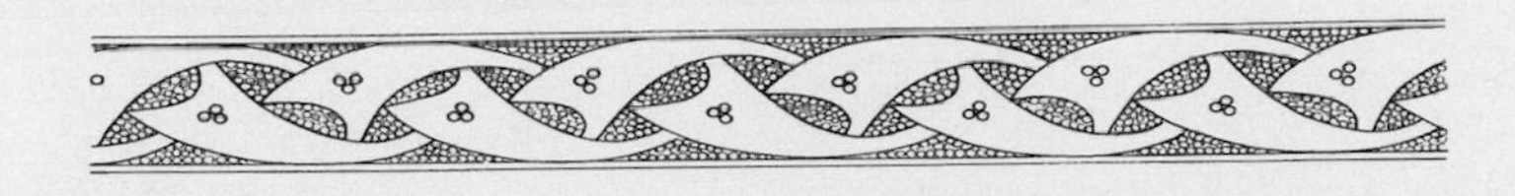

Dancing in the First Advanced Civilizations

The first split of dancing into a rulers' dance and popular dance took place in Egypt at the time of the Pharaohs and in Crete—namely in the first class societies of antiquity. The social class partition gave birth to an "advanced culture" of dancing.

Dancing played a special part in the Cretan-Mycenaean culture (1600-1200 BC), because rites of worship were still very much part of everyday life. The matriarchal influence could be felt in many ways in those societies: goddesses were revered, women held powerful social positions, and their participation in dances contributed greatly to shaping the cretan dancing culture.[8]

Cretan dance was known for its liveliness, its women dancing with loose, flying hair, with the rhythm moving the whole body, right down to the fingertips. Cretan men were also famous for their dancing. Common people were not the only ones to try to reach a certain level of perfection in their dancing; the nobles, too, considered it to be a serious occupation. The flexibility and the agility gained through the dance helped them skillfully dodge enemy arrows.

At the same time, Egyptian culture showed the first signs of a separation between worship and social life. The transition from matriarchal to patriarchal society was taking place and this was reflected in the dancing culture. During official events, dances came to be performed mainly by the ruling class, kings, and priests, while women were only allowed to dance for the entertainment of the higher social classes. Women's loss of social power manifested itself in their restricted freedom of movement as well as in the new functions of their dances. For the first time, we find evidence of professional dancers, girls and women, performing for the entertainment of others, which further demonstrates the transition from the sacred to the profane, to dancing as a show. Ritual dances involving the whole community were replaced by entertainment dances performed by professionals.

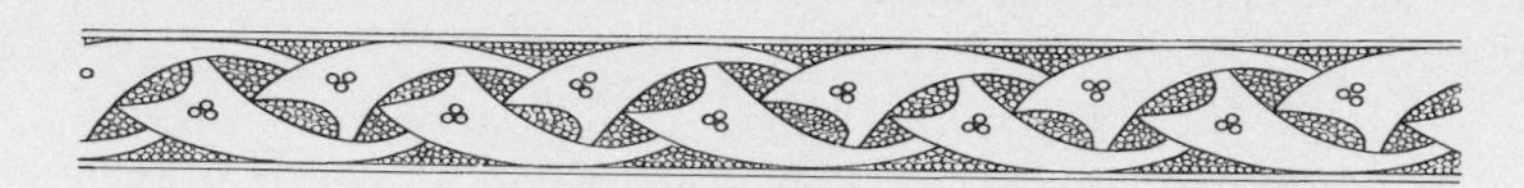

THE GREEKS

Already at the time of classical Greece, women's subordinate position could be seen in the fact that the strong patriarchal structure had nearly completely done away with feminine, self-confident dancing. Fertility dances survived, however, and still included circling movements of the pelvis, swinging of the hips, and shaking of the buttocks.

The Greeks ascribed great importance to dancing. On the one hand, dancing was meant to develop the body harmoniously and teach aesthetic movement sequences; on the other hand, the physical exercises that were part of dancing served mainly as a preparation for war. In a society that worshipped military power, perfection could only find expression in its male representatives. In other words, to quote Socrates: the best male dancers were also the best warriors. As dancing became increasingly formal, "the dancer's own mind and will disappeared. Individual expression gave way to a stricter uniformity while the dancer moved like a puppet, its strings pulled by an invisible master."[9]

We distinguish the following types of Greek dancing: the warriors' weapon and march dances, reserved for men; the religious dances, including women's dances in worship of Demeter and other earth divinities; private dances performed at burials, births, weddings, and other celebrations; and finally, other folk dances.

By and large, except at private celebrations, the increased formality and standardization affected mainly the women's dances.

Women's inferior social position is evidenced by their division into two categories: on the one hand, the honorable, virtuous, decent citizen, unsuited to intensive body movements and on the other hand, the sensual, erotic hetaera or prostitute whose dance integrated the movements and positions of the old fertility rites that had been characterized by wave-like movements of the hips and belly, but without their religious meaning. The prostitute showed off her physical charms for the entertainment and pleasure of her male spectators. Although the women's dance retained many original elements, it lost its sacred meaning when it aimed solely to satisfy male curiosity, a change which has survived to a large extent to this very day.

"Dancing Maidens, Ancient Greece"

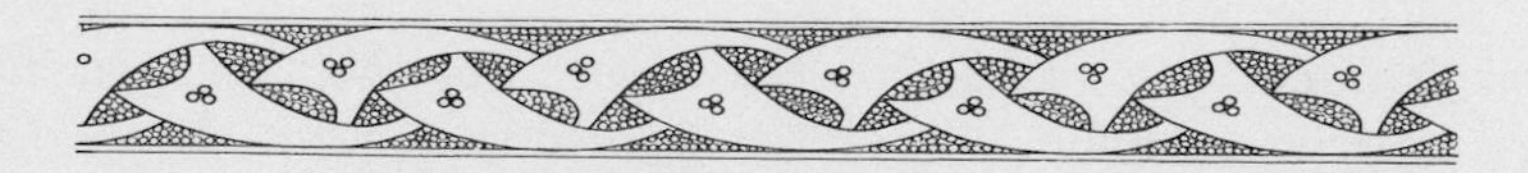

THE ROMANS

Sacred dancing rituals and ecstatic dances were not given any significant tradition in ancient Roman civilization. Dancing was largely excluded from all rites. It was only as Greek political power began to wane that Etruscan and Greek dances found their way into Roman culture, essentially in celebrations honoring Bacchus.

Under the Roman Empire (27 BC to 476 AD), dancing, especially mime dancing, underwent a significant change. The "spiritualization" of dancing through the dramatizing influence of mime corresponded perfectly with the Roman culture of the mind, in which all physical ecstasy had long been banned from public life.[10] The dances performed by the upper social classes were highly intellectualized, while the ritual and worshipping elements survived in the dances of the lower classes. Overall, the Romans gave little importance to the body and kept a distant attitude toward it. Under certain conditions, the body was even considered a prison or a punishment for the soul. A man's social standing was no longer measured, as with the Greeks, by physical and spiritual perfection, but now depended on his wealth, his ascent, his political success, and the number of his children.

The place of dancing reflected Roman society's exclusion of women from the economic and political scene, the restrictions imposed on their freedom of movement, and their physical submission to the ruling powers. Prominent, respectable Roman citizens saw dancing as a source of entertainment and sensual pleasure. The most celebrated entertainment dancers were imported from the city of Cadiz, a Phoenician colony before the Romans finally conquered it. The dancers from the city of Cadiz were famous for "their wild moving thighs and their soft and smooth hips," according to the enthusiastic description of the Roman poet Ovid. Dancers who performed sensual movements to the sound of flutes and castanets were also imported from Syria. In the fourth century AD, 3,000 foreign dancers are said to have lived in Rome.

The gradual disintegration of the Roman Empire led to a loosening of the patriarchal code of morals and customs, so women gained a certain amount of social space. Little by little, they pushed themselves into society and politics and took over the dancing scene as professional dancers. All in all, this did not amount to actual equality, since the increasingly sexually provocative features of dancing reduced the feminine body to an object for the satisfaction of male curiosity. As women turned into the fleshly embodiment of everything repressed and prohibited, they became the polar opposite of the bearers of patriarchal power.

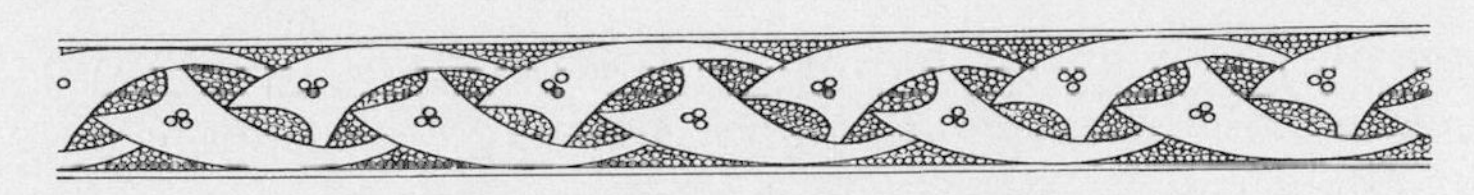

Christianity

The transition from the pagan to the Christian era and the expansion of Christianity in the Mediterranean gradually transformed the Hellenistic-Roman civilizations. For the first two centuries AD, the fathers of the Church retained a positive attitude towards the body. They took a holistic view of human life: the flesh was an animated body to be treated with appreciation. People were seen as whole; their physical existence was part of being a creature of God.[11] This positive attitude was based on the then official interpretation of the Bible. It was therefore logical for the Church to support dancing as well as the physical education of the young.

Yet the end of the second century AD would witness a new trend, characterized by body-hating and the negation of all desires. Experts began to contend that the only way man could find his way back to God and save his soul, was through morality and pure reason—and the negation of the body. As a result, the human being was split into body, mind and soul, with the body damned as the seat of all desires. St. Augustine's doctrine of original sin fostered the belief that women were the bearers of all sins and therefore incarnated sinfulness. The ruling classes' official attitude towards dancing changed constantly until it was finally condemned by the Christian moral code. The Catholic Church, the major political power throughout the Middle Ages, saw in the worshipping rituals of dancing a great threat to the newly-born moral code that denied all physical and sensual pleasure. The sacred aspect of Eros, namely the union of sexual and spiritual energy, was incompatible with their teachings. This is evidenced by the aversion voiced by the Church toward all forms of dancing. Ritual dances were seen as the spawn of evil.

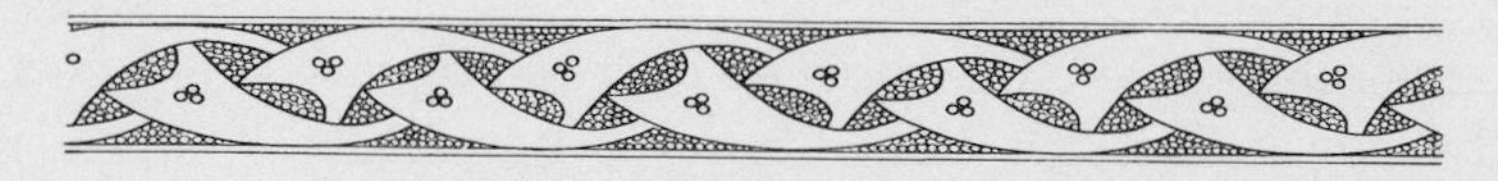

THE MIDDLE AGES

Europe played a minor historical role during the Middle Ages—particularly until the twelfth century. Advanced civilizations were then to be found in the Islamic world and in the Byzantine and Chinese empires. The Western world, product of a disintegrated, barely recognizable Roman empire, strived merely to keep free of the hordes that threatened to swamp Europe in successive waves of invasion. Western Europe was not to revive before the twelfth century.[12]

Although the Middle Ages cannot be described as one single era, a number of basic common features can still be established. Since the sixth century, at the time of limited central social power, the Church had been setting the norms defining the suitable handling of one's own body and acceptable relations to the other sex. The new family structure of the Middle Ages influenced the conduct between the sexes. The clan-family of the early Middle Ages saw the individual as one link in a chain. Sexuality, inasmuch as it was part of an institution, furthered the ancestral chain. An equal spouse was important, since an individual's worth and social status were inherited. The receipt and acquisition of land—that is, power—were also attached to the wedding ceremony, which explains the tight control exerted by the clan over a sexuality that could not be freely lived, with the exception of inconsequential sensual passion. In the late Middle Ages, the household family was to a great extent free of the demands for continuity and strived more for an exchange in the present. Noble descent was still allowed to unite with common wealth, but social control came less from relatives than from public opinion, which demanded that individuals lead their lives in perfect monogamy and in accordance with their stations. Still, marriage in those times showed some constant features. It was controlled by the man, as the bearer of public life. A woman's area of responsibility had more to do with what was wanted from her than with her own personal needs.[13]

The peasant wife was mercilessly worn by the worries of daily survival and certainly did not expect to live in luxury; hunger had to be satisfied before sexual needs. Even so, she could still seem a matriarch to a certain extent, especially given the considerable surplus of men in the country—in the villages of the Abbey of Saint Germain des Prés, in about 820 AD, the ratio was approximately 132 to 100.

A woman mattered clearly a good deal more in peasant circles than in higher, specialized social communities. It is hardly surprising that she would suffer from discrimination if she belonged to either the nobility, where praise went to a warrior's strength, or the middle classes, which needed commercial labor and craftsmen. A woman's single aim in life could be but marriage.[14]

In the Middle Ages, there was a surplus of women in the cities, as for instance in 1449 in Nuremberg where the ratio was 100:88.[15] Given those circumstances, women turned into cheap, untrained labor and became the objects of male sexuality. Prostitution was often the only way for women to earn a living, which came to reinforce the view that she was indeed man's temptress and seducing Eve. Marriage, then, became a woman's life insurance and a man's burden. A woman's only alternative was the convent.

Toward the end of the late Middle Ages, social discrimination against women, which was based on the legal system and on the family structure, led to witch-hunts in which countless women were tortured and killed. After the witch-hunts, all dancing and singing was prohibited by the Church. Despite all bans, ordinary people kept their dancing rituals, especially during social events.

From the eleventh century on, society underwent many changes. The population increased, larger areas were devoted to agricultural purposes, new means and routes of transportation were invented, and the cities grew as a result of the division of labor into manual work and commercial production.[16] The body became the focus of attention, but this time essentially in terms of its ability to produce and its fitness to fight.

Chivalry became part of the ideology of the modern upper class. Upper class women, who were still considered to be man's property, suddenly became idealized and worshipped. But this reverence was paid to an image alone, and so did not lead to any improvement in women's living conditions. Noble women appropriated those masculine projections and internalized the new value system of courtly love. In doing so, they helped create the image of a Christian, moral, and virtuous woman, which simultaneously shaped the new masculine ideal of the "gentleman." At the same time, a process started in the upper classes that aimed to dampen desire and control the body, which led to increased reserve between the sexes—at least in public. The upper class thus distanced itself from peasants, who involved their bodies more freely when relating to each other. Of course, this had clear consequences for dancing. All vigorous movements were eliminated from the "dance of the refined class," which restrained itself to couples dancing. The dancing couple only held hands —duly gloved at that—while fashion both enhanced the feminine form and seriously restricted women's freedom of movement. The dances became more and more stylized, and the distance at which men and women held each other greater and greater, until only hands and heads still moved. It was quite different in the lower classes, where the peasants' and workers' wide, shapeless clothes still allowed the wildest dances.

At the time, it was mainly gypsies who brought the lively, sensual, and earthy pelvic dances from Asia to Europe. Hunger and a tough life had driven them from India to the West since the beginning of the fifth century. Some came to Europe via Afghanistan and Turkey, others through Egypt and Spain. Music, songs, and dancing lay at the center of the lives of the gypsies, whose famous nonconformity and challenge to Western values excited much hostility. To this day, these songs and movements are passed from one generation to the next.

They used their skills partly to mock the demands and values of the elegant society that they entertained. Whenever the gypsies (Roms, Sintes, and others) settled in a given culture, they adapted the latter's folk music and dances for their own use. And so their dances kept changing under the influence of each culture they came across. The West first knew about Oriental belly dancing through these gypsies and the Moors, who came from North Africa and Arabia, and ruled Spain from the eighth through to the thirteenth century. It cannot really be said that belly dancing is the product of one particular culture or tribe; it is a mixture, carried by a century-old knowledge, that has developed within certain social and historical circumstances. The only certain thing is that it has retained its strength and influence throughout all times.

The gypsies' influence on dance is also apparent in other countries. In agricultural Egypt, professional dancers are to this day called *ghawazi*—the word also commonly used in reference to gypsies. *Ghawazi* means intruder or outsider, because gypsies always lived on the margins of society. The important part they played as professional dancers in Turkey also can be seen in the old Turkish name for a dancer, *cengi*, which is believed to come from the word *cingene*, or gypsy.

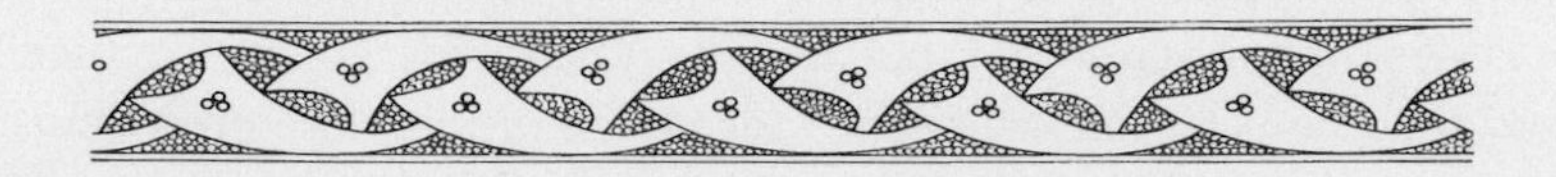

THE ARAB WORLD

Although the fertility dance and its initiation rituals, which celebrated the Great Goddesses of earth, food and life, were indeed repressed in the areas where this religion was banished, they were never quite forgotten.

The women's dance went through a phase of amazing development on the

North African coast, in the countries east and south of the Mediterranean, as well as in the deserts of the Near East. In the Arab world, the women's dance developed both in terms of variety and level of artistic skill. Without any conscious connection to the old fertility dances, it nevertheless retained the same powerful expression.[17]

The attitude of the Arab world to the dance of the feminine pelvis was always ambivalent. Islam disapproves of mixed dancing; a dance that radiates such strong erotic energy and furthers the feminine sexual force should simply not be performed in public. While acknowledging the power of the feminine, Islam sees it as a potentially disruptive factor, unless it be controlled by rules and regulations—hence the use of the veil, the segregation of the sexes, and the practice of isolation. There are but few literary references to belly dancing and whatever exists never describes the dance itself, but instead the sensual fascination it exerts on the spectators.

In the meantime, the women went on practicing the dance of the feminine pelvis among themselves; they did it for their own pleasure and used it in their daily lives and in their ceremonies. For as long as the dance had been part of a religious ritual, no male audience had ever been allowed. Now this separation was enforced from the outside.

Dancers who performed in public were mostly poor women, who did so to earn a living, and often engaged in prostitution too. The poorest among them danced in market places, while the luckier ones were allowed to perform in more aristocratic houses. So most public dancers came to be regarded as prostitutes, and their dance less as an art than a means for the dancer to improve her material station.

From the seventeenth through the nineteenth centuries, Persian miniatures show professional dancers' costumes as floor-length, bright garments, worn over wide trousers with a belt or a scarf tied around the waist. In the nineteenth century, the costumes changed under the influence of European ballet fashion; at the Persian court, dancers began to wear knee-length skirts with transparent blouses. From that point, restrictions faded as the clothing became always more scanty.

The fame of a professional dancer depended on the social status of her audience. Those who danced for a wealthy elite were respected and often quite well-off themselves. It was quite different for those who had to mix dancing and prostitution to earn a living. They lived mostly on the margins of society and only married within their own tribe. They often fed and supported their whole family.

One of these tribes was the Ouled Nail, who lived in Algeria, in the Stone Sahara. Their name can either be taken to mean "Nail's Children" or "Children

Private collection

Syrian Musician, 1890

of the Plated Shoes" (iron-plated shoes or sandals), for they stamped their feet while they danced. These women were taught to dance as children. At age twelve, they would leave their tribe for other places where a new life started for them. They usually lived with an older woman and travelled from one oasis to the next, dancing in coffee-houses and plying a double trade as dancers and prostitutes. Once they had gathered enough money, they would return to their tribe, marry, and teach their daughters to dance. No wonder in those tribes the birth of a daughter was cause for great celebration, since it was the girls who brought prosperity to the family.

This tribe's dancing reflected nature's own rituals. It consisted of forward and backward sliding steps, mixed with a wild footstamping meant to awaken the spirits of the earth. Intense and rhythmic movement of the belly and hips were integrated in the dancing sequence. Hands and arms described the movements of symbolic fertility dances that tried to connect above and below, the one and the many, the eternal and the ephemeral.[18] Their shrill trilling pierced the dancing of the Ouled Nail.

Like all professional dancers, the Ouled Nail wore all their worldly possessions in the form of jewelry. Whatever gold coins they had were sewn to their belts and accompanied their dancing. They liked to wear wide, silver arm bangles studded with pins and points, which protected them against thieves and attackers. Their many layers of ample, embroidered garments with wide sleeves were draped and fastened with silver buckles, on which hung amulets and talismans against the evil eye. They dyed their hair red with henna and wore crown-like caps made of cloth or brass adorned with hanging chains that swirled around their faces. Kohl enhanced their eyebrows and rouge their cheeks. This gave their faces a mask-like, otherworldly aspect. Until the beginning of the twentieth century, the Ouled Nail were found throughout the Maghreb and their name became identified with all dancers, sometimes even those who did not belong to that particular tribe. Westerners took their belly dancing, which was strongly associated with prostitution, to be the original one.

As in all societies, there is a striking contrast between belief and practice in Arab society. The Islam of the scholastic theologist censored music and dance altogether, despite recurring theological discussions questioning the universal validity of this view. Yet philosophical-spiritual movements, popular faith, and numerous mystical schools used music and dance as a "path to the divine origin" of humankind. In this context, dancing is used to dissolve and heal the self; it does not serve as distraction, but as the means to an end.

A woman's pelvic dance with less visible erotic power than the original, has found its home as a folk dance mainly in agricultural areas, where it is a part of all rituals and initiation celebrations. It has always been accepted there. Known by the name of *raqs baladi*, literally "native dance," its presence is particularly strong in Egypt. The "native dance" is an earthy, feminine dance in which the pelvis and hips play a major role, while the arms and upper body are hardly used. There is hardly a social event to which it doesn't belong. No wedding, circumcision ritual or family festivities could take place without this dance.

A professional dancer, on the other hand, will usually perform the *raqs sharqi*.

This dance, called "Eastern dance" in its home country, is based on the *baladi*. It has integrated further elements drawn from other dancing traditions: Indian, Persian, Turkish, and lately the Western ballet. It is widely acknowledged as classical Arabic dance, as it is the most cultivated and subtle form of all. In this dance, the upper body, as well as the arms, hands, and head all bring their graceful contribution. While the pelvis follows the drum beat, the upper body, arms, and hands underline the melody.

Although professional dancers are seen to this day as disreputable in Arab countries, there are enough professionals who try to show the depth of their dancing, to raise it from the nightclub to the artistic level. Still, a dance such as belly dance, which is carried by women's sexual force, life experience, and self-confidence, will always raise objections and discussions, at least until such time when feminine wisdom and maturity are fully accepted and seen as an existential balance to masculinity and a pre-condition for harmony on earth.

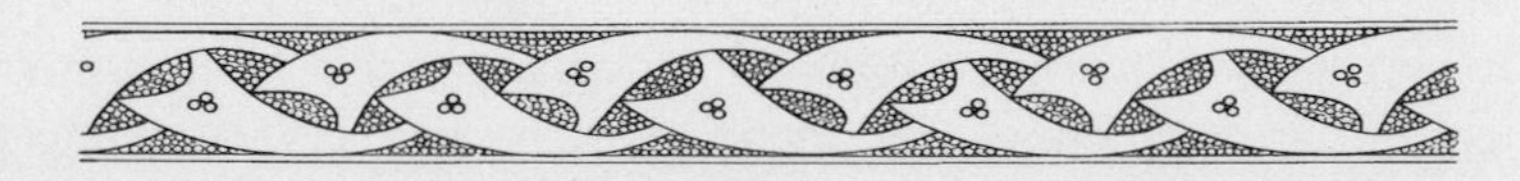

THE BOURGEOISIE

The thirteenth century saw the development of the urban culture of the bourgeoisie, which started in northern Italy and spread to Holland and other countries. The first migrations from the countryside contributed to the weakening of the economical power of the Church. The many discoveries and wars that marked this period led to inner social disintegrating tendencies and to the rejection of the ecclesiastical and feudal representations of the world. A longing to satisfy desires and enjoy the body spread. As a result of the wars, a surplus of women made their way to the cities, where they found work in the crafts. They created their own guilds and female religious communities. They were also active in small business, where they specialized in selling remedies, magical potions, and charms.

The healing arts were traditionally reserved for women, whose knowledge about the effects of plants and juices, obstetrics, contraception, and abortion had been passed on for generations.[19] But they would soon lose their social liberties and relatively equal participation in the production process, because "...their primitive communistic collective thinking and autonomy presented a very real threat to the 'sacramental-hierarchical' structures of business and Church."[20] They were accused of being witches and heretics who were by nature insatiable in the pursuit of their sensual desires—and they were prosecuted accordingly. Their knowledge of natural healing processes was described by the new scientific medical practitioners as barbaric.

Still, the medieval value systems and structures of dependence were unavoidably disintegrating, which gave rise to countless hopes and anxieties. This phenomenon is reflected in the dance forms of that period. In some areas, people literally went into a dancing craze, as a reaction against the repression of the desires imposed by the medieval system of rules, and in an attempt to free themselves from the anxieties and constraints generated by that system. The population was nevertheless still deeply divided along social lines. Just as the lower classes tried to free themselves through ecstatic dances, the bourgeoisie set out to discipline[21] their bodies ruthlessly and adopt the nobility's dance culture. This is how the hostility toward the body and sensual pleasures that had originally been confined to ecclesiastical preaching, grew into a seemingly self-imposed effort to discipline and master the body. The increasingly geometrical approach to the body, and beyond that, to space itself, found its way into the movement patterns of courtly dances. It would later extend to ballet and the bourgeoisie's ballroom dancing. From that time on, the wild movements of dancing were considered primitive and even dangerous, because they aroused the senses and did away with inhibitions.

Overall, one can say that this hostility to sensuality resulted in a new posture of the body, whose gravity center shifted from the belly to the chest area. This "elevation" made it possible for the body to appear light, released from its connection to the earth, while the variations on movements of its extremities multiplied.[22] Breathing became confined to the upper part of the body through the contractions of the belly muscles. This bearing was deemed to reflect dignity and aristocracy.

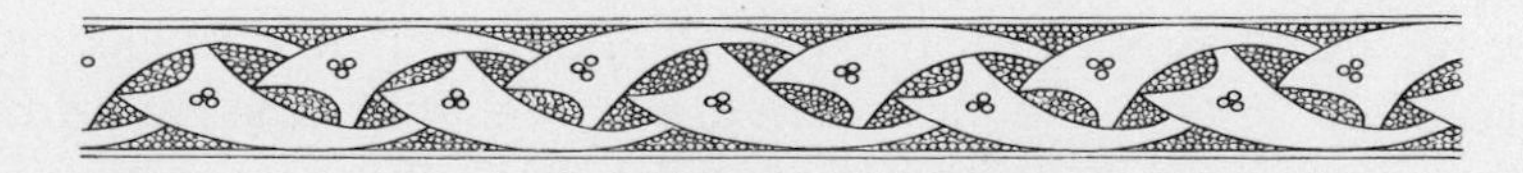

INDUSTRIAL TIMES

During the eighteenth century, the advent of middle-class industrial society, combined with the rise of capitalism and technology as well as the accompanying ruthless exploitation of nature, strengthened the demands for a self-disciplining individual. The invention and above all the widening presence of clocks increased man's independence as well as his alienation from nature.

The subjective sense of time and the sensitivity to individual rhythms, which were based on faith and a feeling of connection to nature, were henceforth replaced by a universally valid, linear, and abstract division of time. With the new "exact" natural sciences and their mathmatical and technical explinations, natural processes came to be seen as created by man, and this created a distance between inner and outer nature. Pure mind began its triumphant progress over pulsions, feelings, and emotions. All and any needs or types of experiences likely to threaten conscious control were viewed with mistrust and fear. The ideological equation of the feminine with nature and physicality, and the masculine with culture and reason, lent a quasi-scientific legitimization to the oppression of women. All distant countries, and nature as a whole, came to be regarded as "exotic women" to be legitimately conquered and "civilized." No wonder that the colonizing nineteenth century regarded the women's dance as a purely sexual, enticing dance.

Life became separated into work and family, whereby the latter was to compensate for man's daily hardships. This brought about internal divisions, especially among the women. As Otto Brunner puts it,

> the split of the areas of production and life (once united in the "whole house") into business and household led to a dichotomy between a "rationality" ascribed to business and a "sentimentality"[23] reserved for the family, the first being understood as a masculine, the second as a feminine domain.[23]

The masculine became the social norm, and the feminine, seen as a deviation from that norm, was devalued and henceforth served to confirm the male norm as its opposite pole.[24] Henceforward, the woman's productive activities within the household were no longer seen as work, but as "natural" fate, from which she was to derive satisfaction and happiness. Any escape or activity outside the home was only tolerated because of social necessities. In addition, women were divided into several ideal types, shaped by men's projections (the romantic, the functional, the provocative, the tomboyish, the child-like) and to which the real woman, as a unique and whole person, could but submit herself. Her own world of experience, her life rhythms, and her inner maturing process, as well as her accompanying changes of identity were totally ignored and categorized into fixed images. The image of the coveted female body, which was hardly ever congruent with its reality, created in women a painful experience of their own body as "imperfect."

Work, discipline, and functionality became the precept for adequate living. As pleasure and lust were driven out of everyday life, after having survived through the Middle Ages, at least in the lower classes, the sensitivity heightened towards all real and symbolic hints of what had been suppressed: more and more, social intercourse was determined by tact, decency and a sense of shame.[25]

As environment and society were measured and put into categories, dancing, too, fell into separate forms: artistic, ballroom and folk dancing.

Still, industrial and technological development brought in its wake, as a reflex, a yearning for an "old world," untouched by the mechanization of life. In the arts, this manifested as nostalgic longing. At the beginning of the twentieth century, a group of women artists, first and foremost Isadora Duncan and after her Ruth St. Denis, drew inspiration from Eastern dances in their search for renewal. Fashion, interior design, book illustration, and stage sets found themselves increasingly influenced and shaped by the Western conception of the Arab world. Although "Oriental belly dancing" was performed on the theater stages of the seventeenth and eighteenth centuries, no true understanding of the depth and meaning of this dance was communicated; it was presented as interesting only because it was exotic and foreign.

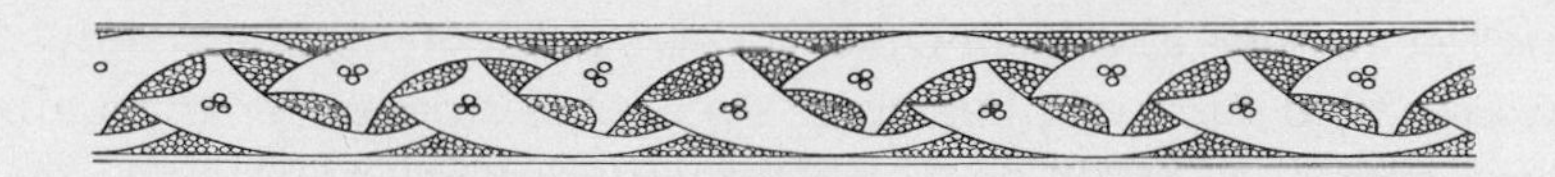

THE PRESENT DAY

At the end of the nineteenth and beginning of the twentieth century, new life reform movements emerged from the rebellious middle class in Europe. These movements stood against the alienation brought about by industrialization, against the plight of the urban masses, against human isolation, as well as against the double split of body, mind and spirit, and the individual, nature and the cosmos. Eastern philosophies and arts were a major source of inspiration.

This struggle to unite human beings and nature, which was first led by the upper middle class, gradually extended to other segments of the population; its latest manifestation is to be found in the New Age movement. A cosmic collective consciousness spread, along with increased individualism and flight into the inner world. The picture of these searchers is distorted by their apolitical standpoint and their refusal to take into account the individual's involvement in history. The one-sided New Age bent toward nature, intuition and irrationality (traditionally feminine qualities) projects on women a kind of redeeming role. Women can save civilization from the dilemma that had led to dehumanization, isolation, and the destruction of nature. The processes are blamed on the dominant male force, which created instability within society and within the life organism. Balance can only be restored through increased female dominance.

The dancing scene witnessed the appearance of new ballroom dances that followed the Afro-American dancing tradition, as well as the birth of expressive dance.

The body culture movement associated with this evolution seemed particularly suited to women's needs. The close connection between body, culture, and femininity was being discovered. A new concept of femininity developed. Dancers like Isadora Duncan took it upon themselves to use their dance to restore women's awareness of the freedom, the harmony, and the inspiration, of the feminine body. On the physical level, this was reflected in a return to the natural and original center of movements, which shifted from the head and the chest back into the solar plexus. These attempts to liberate women were, however, coupled with an insistence on traditional functions, feminine modesty and virtue, as well as the social conditioning of the feminine body.

In the 1920s, women started to seek their identity outside the prescribed male and female roles and to shun the coercive side of feminine identity. Some women managed to strengthen their social position either through their profession, specialized training or artistic activities. Self-confidence, material independence, participation in sports, and sexual liberation all became standard for women. The creation of a tomboyish feminine model was announced. Having exercised away their full curves and inviting hips, women dressed to underline the new straightness of their bodies.[26] They had adapted to male standards. The pendulum swung back.

It was at that time that Arab artists came to look for work in the West. Their arrival triggered a wave of interest in the exotic and the Oriental that only superficially related to reality. A whole film industry developed around the Oriental theme. Theater plays were produced and famous Western dancers studied the "exotic women's dance." Short films such as *Danse du Ventre* and *Passion Dance* (1896) were produced, as well as theater plays such as *Egypta* (1910) by Ruth St. Denis, and films such as *Intolerance* (Hollywood, 1916), a dance film about Babylon, and *Salome* (Hollywood, 1918).

The influence was not only one way. Arab dancers began to incorporate Western dancing in their performances. Several European musical instruments joined bands that originally had counted only four or five musicians. Gradually a whole orchestra grew around the dancers. Arab dancers also started wearing either ballet

Arabesque collection, New York

Agnes de Mille as an Ouled Nail dancer
1920s photograph

shoes or high-heels. The dancing that used to be performed in a highly concentrated, nearly meditative and inward state, thus requiring little outside space, now took on a more extravagant and extroverted turn. Dancers whirled across the room, standing on their toes and making more use of their extremities. Their costumes adapted to the Western image of the Oriental and became exotic and seductive, with excessive splendor and jewelry. Hollywood film costumes were but one step away, and so was the entry into the world of cabaret.

In Europe, social poverty and dissatisfaction lead to a real dancing craze in the period between the two world wars. Dances with strong African or Arab influences such as the shimmy and the Charleston were used to shake away disillusions and social pressures. People now danced in an anticonformist and erotic fashion, in harmony with the body's "natural" movements. The middle of the body and the pelvis became the main centers of movement.

In the seventies, the rationale behind women's professional activities started changing slowly. Western women no longer left their homes out of economic necessity alone, but to acquire both professional identity and prestige. The new women's movements went along with this development. Generally, this movement chose not to emphasize the "natural" differences between the sexes; biology did not necessarily mean destiny. These feminists called into question the artificiality of professional divisions between the sexes and shook the very foundations of society.

Dancing, and above all expressive dancing, acquired a new holistic touch. Human beings were judged and seen in the light of the reality of their daily life and their place in the cosmos. The distinction between private and public should be abolished—this was the slogan of the 1968 demonstrations. And so, that most private of realms, the body, became more visibly and intimately connected to the life of the body politic. Suddenly, the dance techniques were no longer as important as the dancers' bodies giving public expression to the emotions, thoughts and psychological realities that set them in motion. And again, women used dancing as a means to discover themselves. The head of the Wuppertal ballet speculated:

> It is possible that women can liberate themselves of social pressures more through dancing than through any other form of art. This would mean that the question is about feminine physicality: It may be that dancing leads women to feel particularly acutely not only their body but also their social captivity and awkwardness.[27]

In their search for an inner identity and for a social definition, women artists, especially dancers, addressed the divide between the sexes. Gender had to be deconstructed in order to enable a new "humanization" of man and woman. As Norbert Servos put it in *Ballet International,* "An explosive joy of life appears to be returning at breakneck speed. The times of economy and sobriety of form seem to be over; a new love of fullness is spreading."[28] Such was the motto of the eighties in dancing circles.

Greater educational and professional opportunities led women to expect to be equal partners with men, but these expectations still contend with the daily experience of inequalities. They clash with traditional stereotypes and patterns of behavior. Feminism may have succeeded in undermining the old regime, but a transitional confusion still reigns for today's woman as she faces possibilities her grandmothers never knew. A new outlook is required, in which the individual and society find their reunification beyond artificial guidelines, and in which man and woman may find themselves and each other.

In this historical phase of searching and testing, dancing has regained its role, long lacking, in the official body of socially acknowledged forms of physical expression.[29] It is a sensual instrument that wants to enjoy life in the here and now. By intensifying the moment, dancing facilitates the development and finding of the self beyond any anxieties about the future or burdens from the past. For life is connected with time. It is an active process which requires inner preparation in order to be able to face or bring about outside changes. Dancing, the intense moment of being, opens and reveals this instant to people, thereby giving them the possibility to understand their needs and desires, their "yes and no" with greater clarity.

Dancing has thus completed its transformation from the realm of the sacred to the aesthetic and artistic and back to a joyful, sensual, and playful instrument for self-discovery. The contents of dancing changed with each phase, always combining with people's immediate physical and spiritual needs. Indeed, the language of dance flows over the socially coded body, and it uses a different logic that can be understood through sensual awareness. Leaving oneself through dancing to enter a world beyond one's control and beyond the personal level—almost flowing between the inner and outer world—contributes to a new and different understanding of the tensions between the different poles of existence. By allowing the mind and the senses, the inside and the outside worlds, to unite, without ever allowing either to become dominant, dancing makes it possible for people to set out on unorthodox searches for themselves, and to experience sexual and social issues in their own bodies. Dance is an art and as such it enables whoever practices it to constantly improve their skills and self-knowledge. And to know oneself is a human being's most essential duty.

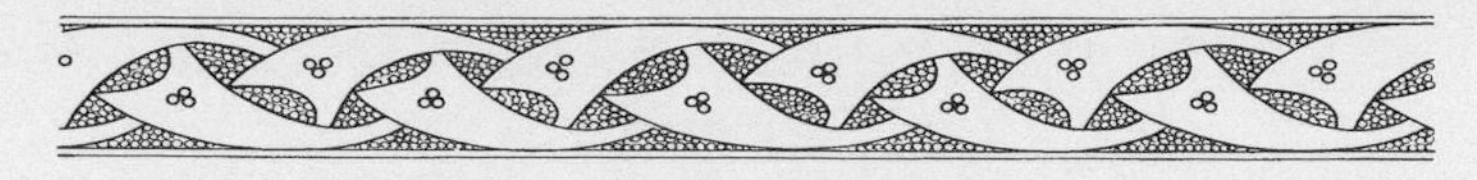

Mother Belly

If we consider a baby's prenatal life in a woman's belly, and we go back to that baby's conception, to the love embrace, to the excited prelude that brought together a woman and a man, we are once again caught in the aroused movement of dancing.[30]

A mother's relationship to her child can be seen as the basis of social life and quite simply the basis of human civilization. Her heartbeat is the baby's first rhythm. Through her, babies experience inside and outside. It is from her that babies receive their first nourishment and are led into life.

As the giver of life and nourishment, woman is the link between birth and death. The feminine holds both. This containing, the most striking feature of the feminine, is expressed positively through shelter, nourishment, and warmth, and negatively through disowning, withdrawing and withholding. Prior to the first advanced civilizations, these two aspects were not separated, because both were understood as necessary to stimulate the capacity for creative transformation.

The representation of the containing female as a vessel is present in nearly all human civilizations. The area that symbolizes the entirety of the containing body-vessel is the belly. The belly is the seat of the inner world, of darkness and of the unconscious, but also of life and emotions. It is the opposite of the breast and head, which symbolize consciousness, the outside world, and light. The upper, breast-head pole rests on the lower, belly pole and cannot be conceived, without this connection.

In rituals, people danced for life, which they saw as the feminine, the Great Mother. This great Feminine embraced the whole world, the good and the bad, upper and lower, life and death. Indeed, life was death and death was life, eternally vibrating, arousing and flowing. To stay in this life harmony, in this aroused moment, to retain this feeling of unity, people danced. They danced for the fertility goddesses, for the food goddesses, and for the hunt goddess. They danced to connect their inner and outer worlds.

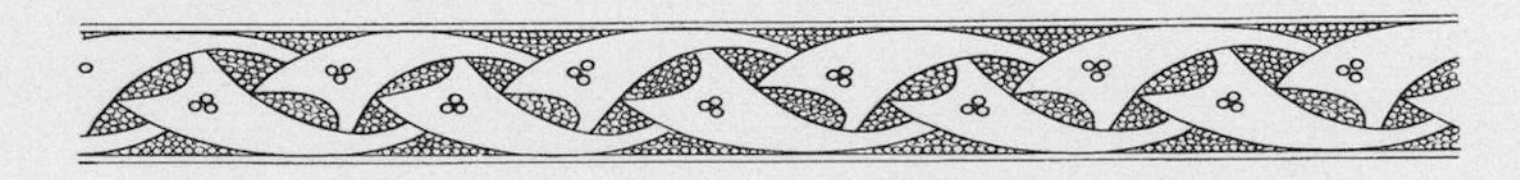

In Praise of Dancing

Body knowledge starts by removing attention from the mind and focusing entirely on movement. Independent thinking, thinking with one's own mind, is learned through thinking in feelings and sensations, and thinking in pictures, free from the rigidity of words. With these two different approaches, a whole world of possibilities opens up.

The movements of belly dancing enable a woman to understand and experience a natural rhythm. In this dance form, she swings her limbs around the center of her body, around the navel of the world, through waves and swinging, rhythmical movements of the pelvis, through movements older than any single woman, indeed older than human civilization. We dance to become one with a rhythm that was here before us and will remain after we are gone.[31]

Through dancing a human being can move beyond limits, into a world of great thoughts where the yearning for transformation lingers and where the majesty of the true self is recognized. With dancing, each human being becomes ancient and universal. The natural ecstasy released through dancing takes the dancer beyond his or her isolation and feeling of being separate. It turns the drop into a river. Dancing is indeed the fastest way to unite with the divine.

In this world full of ephemeral things, wisdom is the one lasting goal for which people can spend their lives striving. And there are as many roads to wisdom as there are human beings. Dizzying, difficult roads, gentle and comfortable roads, and slow, beautiful roads that invite one to linger a while. There are solitary roads and there are social roads, misleading roads and cul-de-sacs, and there are straight roads. Dancing is the most direct way to become aware of your inner space and of the space outside your body. Dancing unfolds feeling, longings, and nostalgia as well as the mind's powers of observation and thought. It is incumbent upon all human beings to recognize their own paths. This duty confers dignity upon them and makes them into noble, honorable beings. The fulfilment of daily chores and duties finds its meaning in the knowledge of one's way. Dancing is a way to find the teacher inside, in oneself. The wings of imagination soar through dancing.

Dancing is the joy of life, of creation, an expression of the awakening soul that is reflected in the dancing experience and in the rhythmic movements. Dancing means building up the body and the spirit, beyond all cultural limitations, uniting human beings with their ancient past, directly yet fluidly. In the heat of dancing, the barriers between mind and body vanish, enabling dancers to grow and plunge into a world of great thoughts and feelings where they find themselves bathed in the fragrance of the transformation for which they have waited all their lives.

Through dancing, people discover the beauty and the strength that lie within; and through the natural ecstasy of dancing, they learn to surrender to a higher force that lets them guess at the unity and wholeness of life. Through their movements, they come to nestle in the movements of the universe and in turn their own movements are reflected in the movements of the stars, the flowers, and the newborn child. Life's burdens and inner turmoil come to a halt in the elevated moment of dancing. In this instant the world becomes a work of art, a kingdom of unity.

Through the intensity of the dancing moment, new worlds and possibilities open to one's own understanding. Through the movements of the body, the heart opens and a great reconciliation with oneself and others can take its course.

In the elevated instant of dancing, human beings experience a feeling of flowing, a childish, playful sensation that enables them to relax into awareness, into a balance between exercising free will and surrendering to the pulse of life.

Through dancing, people understand their feelings. They are moved by feelings of lightness and happiness that enable them to take life easier, to overcome its ups and downs with a lighter foot. Through dancing, people free themselves from the certainty of death and connect to the pulse of life. The barriers between I and Thou become less marked; the methods by which we accommodate reality to our own mold lose their rigidity. The painful coincidence of free will and destiny can be grasped in its greatness, which helps us become children of nature. Free choice and surrender can both be expressed through dancing and turned into intuition.

Intuition, so hard to put into words, is generally considered a "feminine" quality, ascribed to the right side of the brain. Through dancing, intuition can grow, playfully, and become integrated with pure reason. A human being becomes a human being through coming and going, through rising and falling, through the silent words spoken by the heart. Women tend to listen to these words more than men. Through dancing they can follow this inner voice with even greater awareness, lending it rhythm and expression.

Dancing also stimulates the unconscious, which in turn leads to a widened consciousness and an expanded personality. Dancng is an element that heightens life and a feeling of wholeness. Belly dancing, so aptly named, leads to the deep, dark cave, to the center of the earth, before flying, in all its pride and life-force, up to the light, to inspiration, and to new awareness. The way to the spirit is found via the body, via the matter. The fact that the word matter itself is already present in the German word *mater*, mother, cannot be but highly significant, although this connection is often neglected in the "logical and male" world. But both elements are complementary. Without them, no man or woman could develop or become fully human. Becoming aware, searching and longing for unity—not uniformity—can help human beings out of the state of separation and isolation, and lead them along the path to unity.

The essential principle that makes such a transformation possible, is the human capacity for love. As Erich Fromm put it, "Love is first and foremost an act of faith and he who can believe but little can also love but little."[32]

When we dance, we can rise above the little self into the world of mythology and have the chance to become one with the human longing to understand life. Our pain and suffering thus become part of a long story, the human story; this comforts individuals and gives them heart. The heart can then soften and give space for love and understanding. People learn to forgive and grow from a state of isolation into the world of unity.

Through dancing, a woman can oppose the splitting between the social and the natural, as well as the taming of her wilder self, which can start early in a male-dominated history. A woman thus learns to name and express the being that lives deep inside her, waiting and longing to be discovered. This is her other, hidden self, the one who does not match norms or expectations, the one who widens her nostrils like a horse to suck in the wind, who roars like a lionness and shamelessly tears her clothes from her body. This one lives mostly in the background, in the dark cave, deep inside the belly, and only seldom surfaces. She is usually spotted when a person says or does something she wouldn't normally allow herself, when something just tumbles out. It happens without one knowing really how it could come to that. Dancing helps you start to heal this inner split. Dancing offers the conscious and the unconscious, the rational and the intuitive, a space in which they may gradually flow into each other. In belly dancing, feelings can surface gently and safely, acknowledged, and win acceptance, so that life may be seen from another perspective.

Two ancient forces live within every woman, two distinct female beings that combine to create the feminine mystery that men find so difficult to understand. While one force is usually soft, understanding, civilized, and human, the other is often just the contrary. Both forces make a woman into a full female, a "round" human being. Clarissa P. Estés expresses it as follows: "The paradox of women's twin nature is that when one side is more cool in feeling tone, the other side is more hot. When one side is more lingering and rich relationally, the other may be somewhat glacial."[33]

This dual nature makes a woman into an intuitive and instinctual feminine creature. When both sides are given expression, life and nurturing, a woman can enjoy all her strength and all her energy, she can rise above the projected split and live intensely in the moment. This is when she is in touch with the two sides of her nature. At that moment, information and inspiration are no longer based on reason and visible things alone, but come from a level beyond common awareness.

Patriarchal societies have forced women into stereotyped roles: the understanding, virtuous, and self-sacrificing woman, or the passionnate, seductive, and frightening woman. Both feminine images are controlled through the body's appearance, attitudes, gestures, and movements. These categories tear up a woman and rob her of her strength. She has to be very careful not to be misunderstood. To be respected and taken seriously, she tries to hide her femininity and constrict her body into an emotional corset. Split into saints and witches, women were at once put above and beneath the reality of life; either way, they were robbed of all real participation in the development and the shaping of society. They were supposed to derive happiness and satisfaction from a peripheral existence, supposedly in harmony with their "natural" role, namely self-sacrifice and submission. Dancing is an opportunity for a woman to look at these facets in a light and playful way, before deciding where *she* wants to stand.

Belly dancing is a dance form in which femininity and spirituality become one. This may be the reason why it is so taboo.

The force leading to social and spiritual freedom comes from the union of the male and female principles. Yet before the feminine can take in the masculine, a woman needs to become aware of herself. Belly dancing can help a woman find her inner strength. It can become the flying carpet on which she will move and reach her limits, discover her world, and feel the joy that comes from the greatest gift: life itself.

It is said that whenever a sound is answered by the soul for which it was destined, the strings of that soul begin to vibrate. Sound and rhythm involve remembering from the depths inside oneself; they take us back to the origin, to the Great Soul and to a time that was before the diversity of forms and manifestations. Every knowledge is recollection. Thus thirst is quenched, hunger sated, and the heart can beat in peace. Whenever the body moves, the heart is moved and human beings dance to each other. By bestowing this function upon dancing we render its true nature unto it; it is an expression of liveliness.

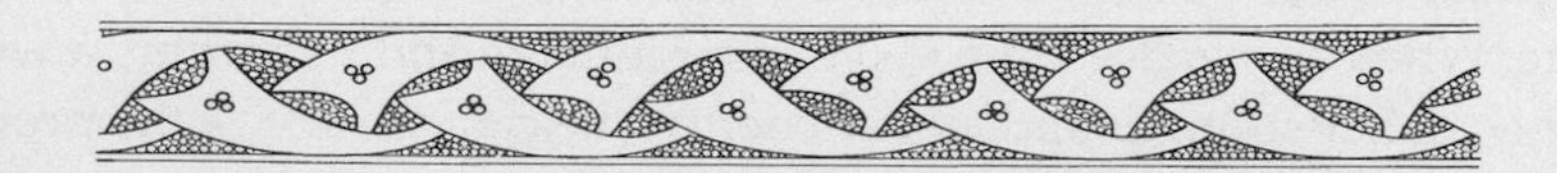

BELLY DANCING

Belly dancing is a dance of isolation, in which the various parts and centers of the body are moved individually, independently from each other, yet end up forming a unity. The polycentric movements of belly dancing develop the body's intelligence and capacity to react, finally resulting in a multidimensional body awareness. Just as individual drops unite in the harmonious flow of a river that time and again draws strength from its source, so belly dancing, as suggested by its popular name, finds its source in the belly. Its rhythm originates from inside, from the elemental sound of the heartbeat that we first heard in the cavern of our mother's belly. If a woman wishes to bring new life into the world, she must have this life force, of which belly dancing is the age-old expression.[34]

Strength for her movements is picked up by the dancer from her belly, the lower part of her body where her balance is centered. She links her lower belly's center of gravity to the earth on which she dances and embeds it in a greater circle of energy. Even her finger movements draw their energy from her belly. And every single movement, however tiny, longs to return to this center. The whole body swings around this center, the navel of the world.

Little space is needed for belly dancing, for its true space is the body itself. The movements of belly dancing are intense and meditation-like, the dancer seeming to be illuminating her inner space rather than needing space outside her.

This dance form quiets the mind and the spirit. Its hypnotic quality induces an inner calm among the spectators even as its movements inspire the senses. Its flowing, round movements and forms are a wonderful balm to the soul.

The movements of belly dancing come from the joints; the trunk finds itself softly kneaded and massaged through its sinuous and circular movements. In most Western dances, the trunk hardly ever moves while the dance is expressed through the limbs. In belly dancing, it is the other way around: the intensive use of the trunk, pelvis, belly and rib-cage strengthens and vitalizes a woman's sexual force. Not only can this force foster new life, it can also lead to spiritual greatness and to a higher level of consciousness. It is of paramount importance for a woman. This force of feminine sexuality is given expression through belly dancing and symbolized through the movements of the dance. Belly dancing gives a woman the possibiliy to discover, learn about, and understand herself. More than words or thoughts, it reveals her attitudes and feelings toward herself and her sexuality, toward men, children and other women. It gives her the possibility to communicate with the eternal woman in herself, to accept herself, and to learn to love. Through the movements of belly dancing, a woman expresses her courage to love and to live. Knowing that the very same movements she is making have been performed by women since time began gives her faith and self-confidence.

In essence, belly dancing is an art of loving. Like love play, it is a mixture of openness and reserve, excited tremor and endless lightness, a nearly unbearable intensity, and a soft sensuality. Although it may appear tremendously wild to the onlooker, it also communicates a feeling of balance and inner peace, close to transparence and fragility, just like the arabesques and calligraphy of Islamic art.

Most Arab women can belly dance without ever having learned it in a dancing school. A certain lack of inhibition with respect to their bodies and their femininity enables them to become absorbed in the age-old movements of moving hips and circling pelvises and to find themselves again.

This women's dance is thus passed on from mother to daughter in the knowledge that it is essential for her body, for her life as a woman, and for her soul. Through their playful dancing, mothers embody the power and strength of feminine sexuality for their daughters. They show each other and they show their daughters how to unfold their sensuality by dancing for other women and by anchoring their feelings and their bodies to life. Through belly dancing, rhythm and expression are given to the joy of being alive and to the joy summoned by new life. Through belly dancing, the women strengthen their daughters' belly muscles, showing them ways to heal themselves as well as a natural understanding of their femininity. It is said that the origin of all weakness and illness lies in the belly. Many diseases may thus be avoided by strengthening the belly. So women become their own doctors and healers.

In North Africa and throughout the Arab world, women sing and dance for each other. The women in attendance support the performer's dance through rhythmic clapping, singing, and drumming. All participate, and a particularly beautiful performance is rewarded and acknowledged by trills and enthusiastic calls. Trilling is achieved by making quick lateral or vertical movements of the tongue while uttering a shrill sound. This is *the* quintessential call of the woman and its effects are both wild and earthy.

Although belly dancing is based on a particular technique, its style is shaped by each individual woman. This is how a woman unveils her personality. Each woman is seen as a dancer, even those who only make a couple of movements before passing the call on to the next woman; no woman feels ashamed if she cannot dance as well as her girlfriend.

In the Middle East, the significance and strength of female sexuality were well-known; it never occurred to anyone to underestimate or ignore it. The attitude toward this sexuality however, was ambivalent. On the one hand, this force was acknowledged and treasured; on the other hand, there was fear about the social chaos it could create. Through veils and isolation, attempts were made to keep it in check. Inside the family, the woman was the seductress, the advisor, and the great, all-encompassing Mother. She was respected and admired and could live her femininity to its fullest. Yet she was only allowed indirect influence on the outside world.

In the Arab world, belly dancing retained its original sensuality. In the West, however, men felt so threatened by women's sexual impulses that they tried to simply ignore them, to neutralize them by tolerating solely "rational" women who were able to keep their strength under control—or, in other words, repress it.

Yet whoever ignores the force of life also avoids the joys of life that are inherent in the body, and all of nature. Such a person will also ignore the other side of life — death. Such ignorance will indeed protect one from the dark depths of life, but at the same time it will also prevent him or her from reaching its peaks. Through the wave-like movements of belly dancing, we can learn to come into harmony with the natural rhythm of the earth. Belly dancing can teach us the courage to overcome our own limitations and barriers that only exist in the world of fear. Inasmuch as belly dancing helps us to explore and experience, we can raise it into a ritual.

So dance, little sister, dance... for as long as you dance, this ancient women's dance will survive and laugh in the face of all attacks. As long as there are women, it will go on beating and living, its proud strength passed on from woman to woman.

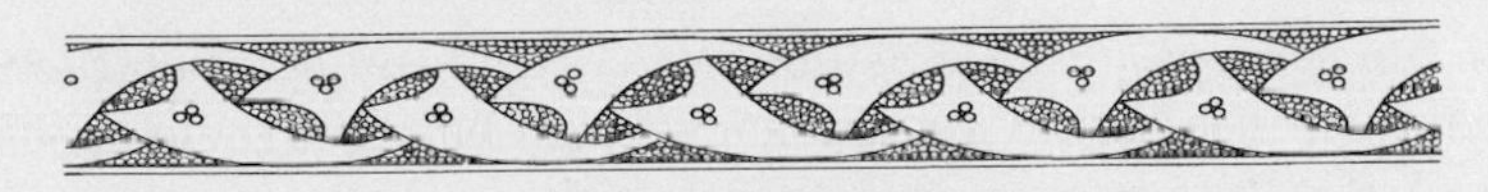

The Basics of Belly Dancing

To understand your body, to be able to make your own diagnoses, you need to be familiar with its anatomy. Many people are barely familiar with their own body functions and fail to realize what happens beneath their own skin, in their intimacy. Yet this is the first step towards wholeness. This chapter proposes to describe the inner body, the relationships between the different body centers and the corresponding dance movements.

The waist is the border between the upper and lower body. The spine supports all organs and balances on the pelvis, which is the touchstone of all movements. The following simplified representation will help you gain a deeper understanding of and feeling for your own body.

From an anatomical point of view, the body has five centers or body cavities: the head, the breast, the belly, the pelvis, and the back. Each center shelters specific organs which connect it to the other centers.

The *head* or *cranium,* contains the brain, the cerebellum, and the brainstem. The cranium is connected to the neck's nervous network, which comes out of the first four cervical vertebrae. This area is stimulated by head circles and swings.

The *breast* or *thoracic cavity,* which is lined by the membrane called the pleura, contains the lungs and the heart. This is the location of the arms' nervous network, which is itself closely linked to the nerves of the heart and lungs. This area is stimulated through shoulder shimmies, all the rib cage exercises, serpent arms, and all movements that entail open-stretched arms.

The *belly* or *abdominal cavity* holds the pancreas, the kidneys, the peritoneum as well as the stomach, the liver, the gallbladder, the spleen, and the small and large intestine. Belly rolls, figure eights and double circles are especially good to stimulate this area. It also contains the solar plexus, which connects the organs of the abdominal zone and is stimulated by belly rolls and fluttering movements of the diaphragm.

In the *basin* or *pelvic cavity* we find the bladder, the sexual organs, the sigmoid colon, and the rectum. Although from an anatomical point of view, there is no separation between abdominal and pelvic zones, differentiating the two makes it easier to understand the whole picture. The pelvic zone is stimulated by pelvic swings and all variations on the hip circle. The pelvic nervous network connects the lower pelvic cavity with the sigmoid colon, the rectum, the bladder, and the gonads.

The *back* or *dorsal cavity* is a long tube located inside the spine and containing the spinal cord. The back is strengthened by all head movements, shoulder exercises and pelvic movements. There are four types of vertebrae: seven cervical vertebrae, twelve thoracic vertebrae, five lumbar vertebrae, and the sacrum, for a total of 25 dorsal vertebrae.

If we try to picture these divisions, we become aware of how belly dancing influences the body and the stimulating effect each movement has on the different centers.

The spine connects all organs through the nervous system and the connective tissue. The nervous system comprises four major nerve zones. On the physical level, the distribution of our vital energy takes place through the spine, which enables the brain to communicate with its "messengers" located in the spinal cord.

The head rests on the spine, which is itself supported by the pelvis. We can thus picture the head as a ball, the spine as a stick, and the pelvis as a seashell on which they both balance. Given that all parts of the body are linked to the spine, the pelvis actually supports the whole body. Each movement is therefore dependent on the flexibility of the pelvic joints. These are moved by the largest and strongest muscles of our whole body, namely the muscles located in the buttocks and upper thighs. The whole body's strength rests on the strength and the flexibiliy of the lower abdomen. Any blockage of the pelvic movements, any hindering of the free movement of its joints—hip joints and small of the back—make a correct posture or movement impossible. A correct movement means that the effort is distributed according to the muscles' respective strength, the larger ones bearing a greater load than the smaller ones. Any movement felt as stressing means that muscles located on the body's periphery (hands, arms, feet and legs) are being mobilized for efforts beyond their capacity. This leads first to major tension in the shoulder or leg areas, and later to cramps and pains that stem from the irregular rhythm of the movements.

By freeing the movements of the pelvis, the spine—and through the spine, all the internal organs—can be stimulated. All forms of meditation stress the importance of a straight spine, whether in a sitting, lying, or standing position. Indeed, the subtle energy which transports an expanding consciousness ascends from the lower extremity of the spine towards the head, over the spine and then out and upwards. The swings, circles, and spirals used in belly dancing stimulate gently and gradually dormant energies, which are then picked up by the body. So belly dancing refines energy and consciousness progressively and playfully, in perfect harmony without any risk of trauma.

This type of dance has yet another gift to offer: the opportunity to express many different selves and to awaken all the archetypal figures that lay dormant in all women: mother earth, flirt, sensualist, artist, healer, imparter of knowledge. To perform belly dancing, it does not matter whether a woman is young or old, fat or thin, socially integrated or marginal. Belly dancing is not a competition—competing is not part of its nature. This dance form is more than just a dance. Only a woman's life experience and sensuality can lend it both meaning and a true depth.

Expressing her personality through belly dancing, at times alone, at times with others, enables a woman to take a new look at her sometimes negative self-image, in a supportive and strengthening atmosphere. This uniting of earth and spirit, strength and grace, intensity and inner peace, sensuality and poetry, enables many a woman to reach inner freedom.

So take your dancing into your own hands, heal and strengthen your body, as many a woman has done before you and will continue to do. Set out on this great adventure with yourself, and discover the universe.

Part Three: From Head to Toe

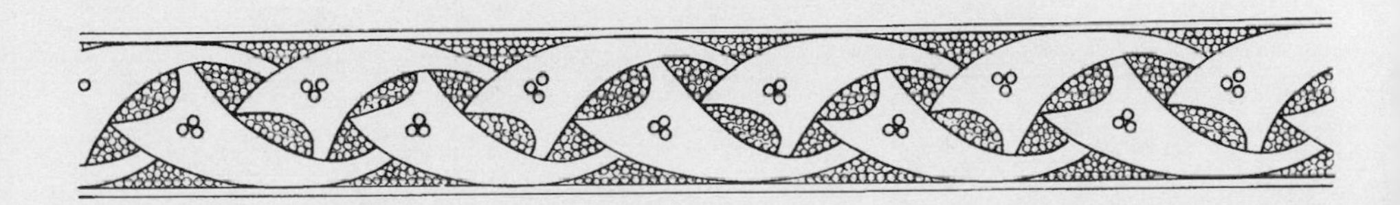

Learning can only bear fruit when one is ready for a smile
and when this smile may at any time break spontaneously into laughter.
Moshe Feldenkrais

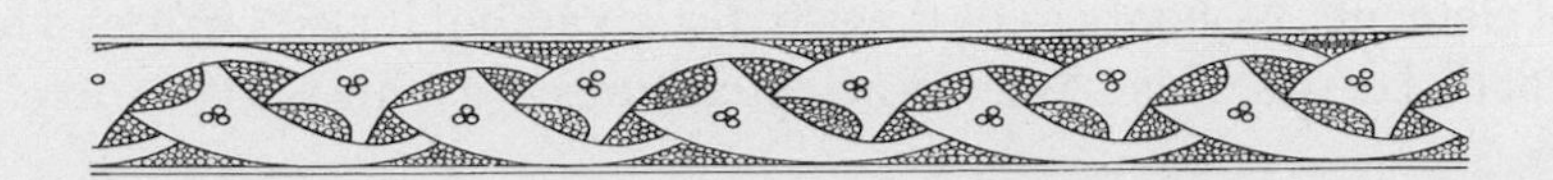

None of the five centers described in the previous chapter can be taken as dominant in belly dancing, yet all strength stems from one source: the belly and pelvis area. The art of expressing moods, states of mind, and experiences through dancing is based on movements and shapes that are meant to strengthen the body, keep it flexible, and prepare the dancer for life.

Another thing: If you wish to attain awareness through dancing—that is to say through any movement—you should progress slowly and carefully, free of any form of ambition, competition, or pressure. Only in this way is it possible to discover your own learning rhythm; only in this way can you truly and successfully learn; only in this way can you discover and gently eliminate all unnecessary tensions. Learning must be enjoyable and easy. This makes for simple breathing. Only thus may you turn the impossible into something possible, easy, comfortable, enjoyable, and finally, aesthetically pleasing.[35]

Many of the movements described in the following sections ask you to take the basic position. To do so, stand upright with your knees slightly bent and the weight of the body well and equally balanced on both feet. Arms are close to the body, elbows slightly bent. You are actually taking the position of a child, with all extremities softly bent and your breathing smooth and deep.

Now raise your arms, anchor your feet to the earth and let your being fill up the space between heaven and earth.

THE HEAD

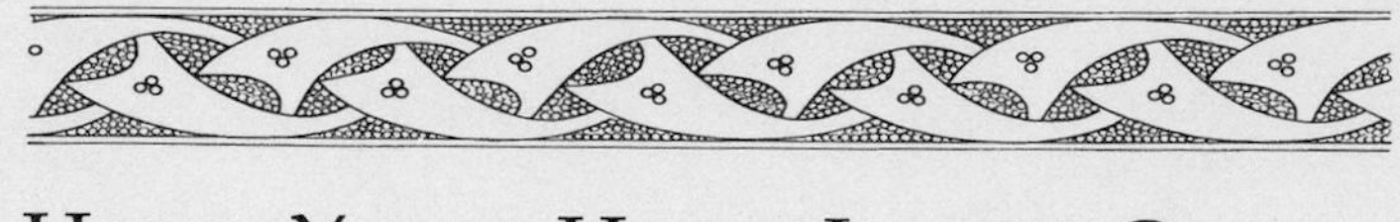

HOLD YOUR HEAD LIKE A QUEEN

Because of its all-cleansing and all-renewing qualities, water is queen among all elements. Not only does it wash dirt away, but it also purifies a human being of bad deeds. This is why, in many cultures, washing is a part of religious rituals.

Stand up and close your eyes. You stand between above and below, between heaven and earth. The above in you is your head, the below your pelvis. A pelvis shaped like a basin, a basin full of water. Now imagine a spring coming out of your pelvis and flowing upwards along your spine, all the way up to the top of your head. When the jet of water pulses right to the top of your head, along each vertebra and through the highest vertebra (the atlas), then your head is in the right position, well-balanced, without any tension rising from the pelvis. Neck tensions usually arise from fear of failing, of making mistakes, from a feeling of inadequacy in a given situation. You will become aware of such tensions. Take the time to repeat this exercise time and again, and when you circle your pelvis, maybe you'll also come to understand the reason for these tensions.

Also, remember that you are often biased in your self-criticism, that you see failures where an objective observer would never find fault.

In belly dancing, the head rests calmly between the shoulders. Held high, it takes on a majestic stance and radiates dignity. This mixture of solemnity and calm, the near indifference and immobility of the head helps the dancer widen and open her chest to leave space for the heart.

This majestic deportment of the head is kept throughout all movements and bears witness to the fact that the woman who dances is aware of her femininity and enjoys sharing this awareness. The head position expresses her courage and the resulting honesty, first of all towards herself.

In Arab countries, women can often be seen carrying bags, jars, and even whole trays on their heads. They walk as gracefully and calmly as if their head were beyond the reach of the rest of their body. The rest of the body can turn and move in any direction, yet the burden never moves. The secret is that the woman is centered in the lower part of her belly and can therefore move her pelvis perfectly freely; consciously or unconsciously, she knows the connection between head and pelvis. Indeed, the spontaneity and lightness of her head movements are rooted in the freedom and flexibility of her pelvis.

With belly dancing, you learn to hold your head high without losing the ground under your feet; without fear of being misunderstood, for it is not arrogance that gives you this strength, but the knowledge that above and below are one, and that you are the daughter of both.

Stand upright and balance your weight on both legs. Now breathe deeply into your belly and put all your weight in the lower part of your belly, until you have the feeling that you are resting, sitting in yourself. If you bend your knees slightly, the position becomes more intense. A tip: try lifting one leg by bending it; this will gradually bring your center of gravity deeper down into your lower belly. Once you can keep your balance, you'll know you have succeeded.

Now imagine that you are carrying a weight on your head and connect it to the weight in your belly, along the spine. Stand upright and try taking your first steps. Put one foot in front of the other, very carefully. Feel your way by putting your toes and the ball of your foot on the ground first, instead of your heels. Try bending your knees now, with this imaginary weight, and come up again; try turning to the right, then to the left; try walking backwards; try to sit. You can use your arms to help you balance your movements. Now try it with a real weight. Find something that won't slide—a piece of material, a cushion or something else not likely to break. Practice as long as you enjoy doing so, and observe how you move and the effect of this head weight on your body and on your movements.

Thoughts can also weigh on your head, yet when the opposite polarity, the belly, is brought into play, harmony and balance cannot be impeded.

Head Slides

This is a particularly stimulating head movement: move your head until it rests on your left shoulder, then let it drop, make it heavy and move it along your chest, until it reaches your right shoulder. Repeat this movement slowly and carefully, until it flows, and you feel: "Now, I've let go!" You can also increase the intensity of this head movement by dropping your head forward and letting it swing from one side to the other. Used above all in the hair dance (see The Wedding Dance, p 141), this movement is especially beautiful when you let your hair loose.

Figure Eights (Head)

Another head movement that you can incorporate into the dance is the figure eight. Bend your head forward and describe a figure of eight in the air,

Andi Diem

Your body is held upright through your head and pelvis.

as you do with the hips (see Figure Eight or Loop of Infinity, p108). Here is a combination: Start by performing a figure eight with your head, slowly and carefully at first, then somewhat faster and suddenly extend it to your pelvis and move your hips in the same way. You will immediately notice how this connects you to the earth.

When you dance, you can let your head accompany your movements. By doing so, you will direct your attention to the part of the body concerned, and thereby accentuate it even more.

Adding a head movement also helps stimulate body intelligence. It is a great art to move arms, chest, pelvis, head, and eyes simultaneously while resting in yourself. A tip: When you smile, it gets easier!

UNRWA

Earthenware jars are carried to the well to be filled with water and life.

THE EYES

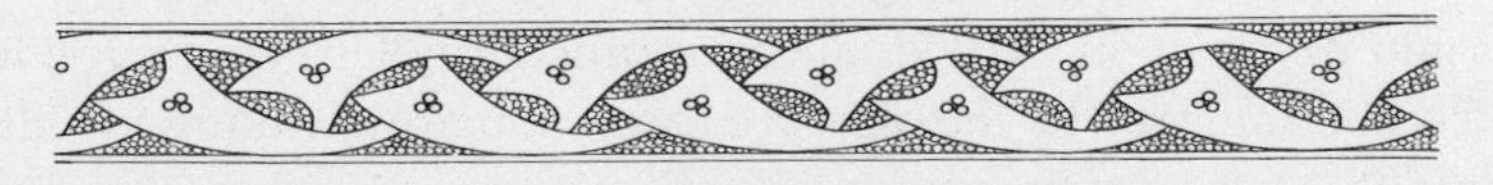

THE OCEAN OF THE SOUL

Sight is one of the most beautiful gifts ever bestowed on human beings. It is through the eyes that feelings come across most sincerely, through them that we can read another's thoughts most intensely. Which is why many people avoid gazing and try to keep their expression as neutral and steady as possible. In the process, the eyes lose some of their beauty, the expression some of its

Holzknecht

Open and alert, the eyes experience all the excitement of dancing.

richness and diversity in individual communication. Use your eyes, let them talk. You will be amazed by the pleasure those you are speaking to will take in diving into this ocean of the soul (with a life jacket to begin with, of course!).

Start by standing in front of a mirror and look into your eyes. If you wear glasses, remove them and observe your eyes. Come closer to the mirror and take your time. You will be amazed by the depth, the liveliness, the questioning, the seriousness of your gaze, as if some hidden part of yourself were looking at you. Now try to let all kinds of moods and feelings show in your eyes: joy, anger, sadness, pride, playfulness, kindness, refusal, care, love, sensuality, hatred... See how your eyes are transformed.

UNRWA

The gaze reflects the soul.

The following exercise will help you improve your eyesight: put your palms near your temples like blinkers, a few inches away from the temples. Now direct your eyes to your left palm, then to the front, then to your right palm and back to the front. Don't move your head, only your eyes : *left – front – right – front*.

Repeat the exercise by looking at the bottom of your left palm, then your right palm.

Imagine a circle in front of each eye. Close your eyes and walk them round the circle, clockwise, then counter-clockwise.

Try to do this while keeping your eyes open, slowly and gently at first, then a little faster. You will be pleasantly suprised by how relaxed you are and how good your eyes feel.

Whenever you dance, use your eyes. Let them sparkle and demand, play with them and let your feelings show in them: first soft and seductive, kind and gentle, then suddenly knowing and searching; look into the distance, without focusing on anyone, then suddenly look straight into the heart; center yourself by half-closing your eyelids, then open your eyes wide and look straight ahead; lean your head to one side, open your eyes even wider and pretend to be shy, worried or coquettish. A whole world of sensations, stories, and contemplation opens.

Exercises

Vision through the third eye can also be improved through exercises. Inner vision helps with questions, as each question is the mother of the answer that lies dormant in your inner self. This exercise will help you see the answer.

You are probably familiar with the stage that occurs just before you fall into the world of sleep and dreams. When you are in this intermediary state, you have already left the outside world, without having yet entered the inner world. Before you lie down, decide to remain on the edge, to stop at this limit. In front of you stretches the dream world, behind you the outer world. Here, in this half-awake state, you can train your third eye, your inner vision. You can ask specific questions, or else stay with whatever is bothering you and just let the pictures form. Don't try to analyze what comes up, just stay in that semi-darkness where both worlds meet and merge.

Usually, at first, you can only remain in that space for a few short moments before falling asleep, but with time and practice, you will be able to extend your stay in this in-between world for as long as you like.

You can also practice with a partner, by lying down side by side and entwining your little fingers. This anchoring can help you remain longer on the edge, balanced beween both worlds.

Here is another way to transport yourself into another mode of consciousness and see the world around you from a different perspective:

Lie down comfortably. Let your body relax, become heavier and melt into the ground. Take a few deep breaths, and focus your attention on the space just above and between your eyebrows. It will fill with warmth and light. A light-drenched carpet will unfold in front of your third eye. Walk on it and fill it with your imagination. Picture it as a place where you feel good. Each movement of your body will fill this space, this landscape of yours. And you are at the center of it. Endless time is yours; you can go at your own pace and take off to any destination. This is your space, your temple, where you can relax and find inner peace, where you can summon up all your creative powers and be yourself, completely.

Whenever the time comes for you to withdraw, go back to the space between your eyebrows and concentrate once more on the feelings you have experienced before regaining awareness of the ground on which you are lying, before stretching and opening your eyes. This exercise can also be done sitting or standing.

Whenever you need to relax and find yourself, you will be able to retreat to this space and quiet your spirits.

The Art of Seeing

Seeing is an art and it takes training. Look out of the window. Observe what you see. Now close your eyes and go inside, then open your eyes spontaneously, get up and look again. What can you see now? Can you also feel what you see? Try again. Can you feel what you see? Yes! And what's happening inside you? Can you feel it when you're looking? When your sight is awake, your whole face lights up, your eyes become calm, and you are supported by yourself and the world, simultaneously.

Concentration Exercise

The following exercise can also be done with a partner:

Light a candle and put it in front of you. Look at the light and let all the thoughts and images that come to you melt away. Don't hold on to anything, don't let yourself be distracted by any outside movement or noise. Concentrate entirely on the flame.

Every two minutes, your partner will break the silence and ask, "Where are you?" Don't answer, just concentrate again on the flame. Repeating this exercise will teach you how to focus your attention and guide your thoughts.

We live in a time in which sight has come to dominate the other senses. Seeing always creates a distance between the observer and observed. It entails a dual approach to the world, in which the observed is always relative—in other words, subjective. The eye is often considered to be a masculine organ because it creates distance and limits. The masculine needs to find a counterpart in order to exist. A boy must thus separate from his mother to develop his masculinity; he needs the "I" and "Thou." The girl *is* the mother; she is close to her and united with her. She doesn't need any separation. If the eye can be described as masculine, might the ear be feminine?

THE EARS

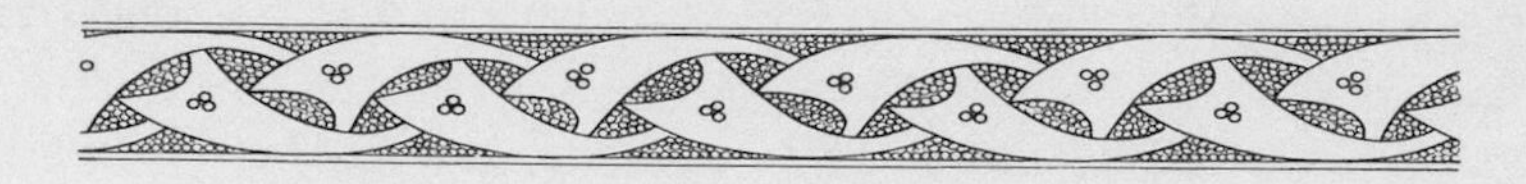

THE GATEWAY TO THE SOUL

If the eyes are the mirror of the soul, the ears are the gateway to the soul. Whenever you feel tired, out of sorts or just in bad humor, put on your favorite music and observe the effect it has on you. Let it draw you out of the spiral of your low mood; in no time, the whirlwind of your thoughts will quiet down and peace will fill your breast.

Put some music on and rub your ears with your hands until your ears feel alert, like two open mussel shells. Stand in the basic position, start circling your hips, and put your hands on your belly. Let the music flow into your ears and guide it along a spiral, all the way down to your belly. Connect your ears to your belly, as it is gently massaged by your circling hips. Fill your pelvis with music; let it flow and submerge you. Feel the music as it fills up your abdominal cavity. You'll become all belly and ears. How do your ears feel? Which ear do you listen with most intently, the left or the right? And how about your belly? Is it changing into a resounding surface for all sounds, all rhythms, relaying them to your whole body? Circle your hips and let your ears become your inner eyes. Learn to see with your ears and listen with your eyes.

Digression: A Commentary on Arabic Music

Despite its many regional variations, Arabic music can always be recognized by its strong rhythmic improvisation and haunting melodies. It draws you inside yourself. Music and chanting cannot be separated from the Arab way of life. Highly praised in certain historical periods and repressed in others, music has always continued to play a major part in countless social and religious events.

Arabic music is distinguished by a modal tone system, which is ruled by the *maqam*. Each of the *maqamat* takes its name from a specific note, which is usually named after a town, a landscape, or even a tribe. Each is based on a scale that incorporates microtones—intervals smaller than the half-steps of traditional Western music—and is developed through vocal or instrumental improvisation. Melodies move in whole tones, halftones or quarter tones throughout the octave, which is itself divided into 24 practically equal parts. In a sense, the melody, which is the arrangement of space, is fixed, for each *maqam* carries with it a typical pattern of melodic movement and emphasized notes.

To get a better sense of this form, compare the *maqam* to the waltz. A waltz is characterized first and foremost by a fixed arrangement, not of space, but of time: the time signature never strays from ¾. A composer creates a melody and sets it to this time signature. The melody is subject to no rules; every waltz has a different one. But the rhythm, the arrangement of time, never varies.[36] In a *maqam*, on the other hand, it is *time* rather than space that is not subject to rules —there is no constant meter, no fixed beats regularly repeated. This creates a feeling of eternity, without beginning or end (though really a *maqam* is based on different basic elements and patterns).

A *maqam* is divided into several melodic registers, each of which is separated by relatively long pauses. Each new register evidences something new, treated separately or in combination with the previous register.[37] It takes a very attentive ear to recognize the internal structure of a *maqam*, especially for one unfamiliar with this kind of music.

Each *maqam* conveys its own feeling and atmosphere and creates a different mood in the listener. The extremely fine vibratory nuances and states of mind induced by microtones can be used to heal psychological and physical troubles. According to a widespread belief in Arab countries, music is said to dissolve self-control as well as blockages, to provoke moods, and bring memories back like no other form of art, which is why it is also used for healing. So *maqam "rast"* induces a feeling of pride, power, spiritual health, and virility. It affects the eyes, the head, and thought structures. *Maqam "bayati"* brings to the fore a feeling of vitality, joy, and feminity. It acts first and foremost on the heart. *Maqam "sigah"* brings about a feeling of love. It influences the liver and kidneys. *Maqam "hidjaz"* evokes the immensity of the desert and of eternity. It is thought to act on the sexual organs. *Maqam "saba"* awakens an intense feeling of sadness and pain. It acts especially on the breast and belly areas. All in all, there are over seventy series of *maqam*.

Whereas Western music abounds in variations, Arabic music is borne by a forever repeating melody, which lends it a hypnotic character. It can be compared to the waves of the ocean, always returning, always different, with the difference always extremely subtle and fine. It takes time to recognize and appreciate these subtleties. Although belly dancing can be practiced with other music, it is particularly well suited to Arabic music, which enhances the feeling of inner space, thus helping the dancer concentrate on her own inner space and inner body movements.

How does this all relate to the sense of hearing?

At the moment of death, when all our senses fade away, when we can no longer feel, taste or smell, the last sense that disappears for most of us is that of hearing—which was our first sense, too. The ear begins to develop on the seventh or eighth day following conception. Four and a half months later,

Andi Diem

The sensuality of dancing starts with the ears...

the internal ear has reached its final size. So a new born baby comes into this world with considerable auditory experience. Having already heard the regular beat of the mother's heart for months, the baby can distinguish between a sneeze and a cough, and knows countless gurgling sounds.

Our hearing center is located in the rock bone, thus named by scientists because it is the hardest bone of the whole human body. No other part of the body is better protected than our hearing center. How important it must be for human development to warrant such protection!

Now, for a moment, travel down your body to look at your feet. Have you ever wondered how it is possible for such small feet to carry such a large body? Standing upright has been more difficult to achieve than developing the brain. Primates have been defined by their upright position for merely the past six million years, whereas the brain developed much earlier. This upright position is ruled by the ear, which is in charge of our balance. This is why the nerve network linking the ear to the spine is much denser than the one linking the eye to the spine. In order for us to be able to stand, our ear must receive information from balance receptors located throughout the body, down to the soles of our feet.

When you fall, it is your ear that protects your body from the fall. The violent commotion that hits the floor of the internal ear provokes a contraction of the falling body, which prevents the back of the head from crashing against the ground and sets the point of impact on the curved spine, near the center of gravity.

Arabesque collection

...and the sound in your ears keeps you walking upright.

This is how the body is able to sustain major falls without lasting damage.

Observe yourself: when you want to listen more carefully, your body straightens up. Animals, too, sit up to hear better. By contrast, seeing requires no activating impulse. Could it be that sight is just a "comfort" sense? When you know that ninety percent of the electrical energy received by the brain comes from the ear and that the remaining senses satisfy themselves with a mere ten percent, the answer is clearly "yes." In a predominantly visual world, this statement gives food for thought. Sight can entertain you, keep you busy and informed, but it does not further the brain's development.

Sounds, music, speech, orientation, and communication are all related to hearing. It is through hearing that the brain and thoughts are activated and conditioned. Because sound waves disappear rapidly, they require fast processing.

This doesn't apply to sight: once seen, a landscape remains, unlike sound waves, which are soon gone. If visual perception determined the functioning of the brain, we would think a lot more slowly, precisely seven times slower, for we can hear seven times faster than we can see.

Why then is the sense of hearing so overlooked?

Speech, the outward beam of sound, fulfills its function when it is returned to the sender. There is a link between the creature who uttered the sound and the one who sends it back. Out of questions and answers, language is born. No mental development is conceivable without this principle, hence the importance of awakening our children's hearing sensitivity.

A question asked begins a sequence. We can think because we are able to ask questions, the answers to which lead us to further questions. Purely visual beings would have little reason to develop a system of questions. They would already know everything they needed, because a totally visual perception of the environment leaves little to be discovered. Anything of immediate importance is instantly recognized. The eye transmits a finite state; the ear takes you further, into yourself, and into the outside world. Should we follow our society's growing emphasis on visual reality, thus remaining in the purely visible, material world? Should we stop asking questions and content ourselves with passive consumption? Trapped in our anxious selves, should we just look at the world through the window pane of our television screens?

Ears don't lie; they perceive things and sounds as they are. Inside and outside unite through hearing: when I listen, I transpose what I hear inside myself and the listener and listened become one. Much more so than seeing, hearing is about taking in. When I look, I am always slightly somewhere else and a distance arises between me and the observed. When I listen, the "sound picture" is assembled in my brain. The whole experience is integrated in the brain's space pattern so that the ears can "see." All the information, waves, and oscillations are transmitted by the ear to the brain in the form of electric signals. It is only in the brain that they are deciphered and become sounds, music, or speech; the "sound picture" is formed in the brain, as opposed to the "visual picture," which is born in the eye, on the cornea. This is why more nerve connections are needed between the ear and the brain than between the eye and the brain. The hearing process transmits the information much more deeply into the listener. Optical illusions are a common concept; although they exist, acoustic illusions do not occur often enough to justify a special term.

What is hearing? What is language? What are questions? Aren't the signals sent out by a living being always questions to itself, however indirectly? And what is silence? Isn't it the interval, the soundless space that transforms a sound into rhythm? What matters is neither the sound nor the beat, but the silent, quiet space that separates them. This is the space, the interval in which I can stretch out. Each sound aims at silence. Silence is the return to the origin. Surrounded by silence, the soul can soar.

And what are thoughts? Thoughts are the primeval mother of sound. Once you start observing yourself, you begin to control your thoughts and you can step out of their ceaseless, trying whirl. You learn to control your thoughts and not the other way round. And what happens then? This is when you can hear silence and the music of the universe starts playing.[38]

If you wish to become more awake, more aware, pay attention to the emptiness between the beats.

Exercise

This exercise aims at stimulating your hearing sensitivity while developing and refining your awareness.

Sit or lie down comfortably, if possible in a natural environment to avoid any distractions. Find two sounds and concentrate on them: it can be the whispering wind, chirping birds, or even your neighbor's hammering or a dripping tap. Once your ear has become tuned to those two sounds and you can distinguish them from all the others, find a third sound. Hearing three sounds distinctly from each other requires perfect concentration, but it can be achieved. Once you succeed, you will realize that you are totally in the present, without past or future, excluding anything superfluous.

Another Hearing Game

Invite some friends and prepare everything in advance so that you won't need to leave the room. Surprise your guests by spending that evening with them in the dark. People gather, they talk, they listen to music, they go into the game of questions and answers—but no one can see the other; hearing is all that counts. What the others look like, their clothes and gestures—none of this matters, only their voices, their silences, their words. By getting to know another human being in such a different way, do you find new worlds opening up for you? Use your ears to picture this person. How do you handle silence? Observe yourself. Or rather, listen to yourself.

THE NOSE

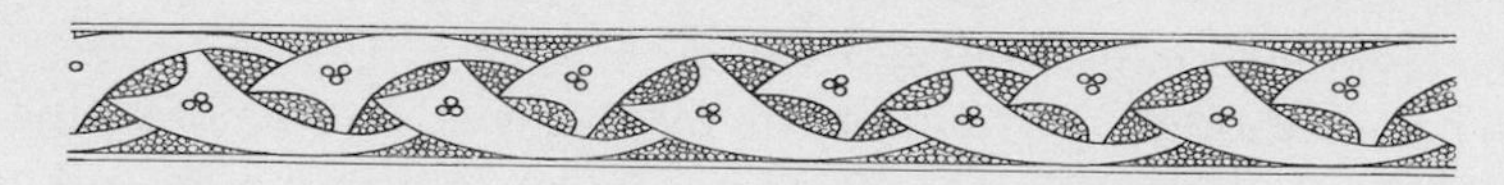

FRAGRANCE, TAKE ME BACK FROM WHENCE I CAME

Whenever you dance, surround yourself with lovely smells. Fill the room with incense and let your nose join in your dancing. The more senses participate in your dancing, the more intense the experience becomes, and the easier the transition to the intensity of the moment, to the here and now.

In the East, no sense is more lovingly cared for than that of smell, which is regarded as the most "spiritual" of all. Memories of past experiences may be called back to life through a scent.

Particular attention is paid to body odors in the East. Before each prayer, Muslims perform a ritual washing of the hands, nose, mouth, face, arms, head, ears, neck, and feet. After every visit to the toilet, the genitals are washed with the left hand. Body cleansing plays a major part in daily and religious life. Furthermore, the importance of fragrances and their effects on the soul are well known. The souk is filled with the smells of spices. Incense burns in shops and homes alike, to pacify the soul as well as the invisible beings, the *djinn*. It is practically a duty for a Muslim to appear sweet-smelling and clean at Friday prayer.

Digression: Six Stations Along the Route to Human Happiness

Mysticism, which is just another word for spirituality, has been described as the "great sacred river that flows through all religions." In the widest sense of the word, mysticism can be defined as an awareness of One reality, whether it is called "wisdom," "light," "love," or "nothingness,"[39] since all these definitions are at best approximations.

In a religion that emphasises divine transcendence—albeit without including, like Christianity, the belief in the incarnation of the Divine—the question of how the creature makes contact with the creator, in other words how people can find their salvation, is bound to be of the utmost importance.

Not unlike the neo-Platonists, the mystics of Islam hold that all creatures emanate from one divine creative spirit, with which they may be re-united after progressing along stages of increasing spiritual enlightenment.[40] The knowledge of this Enlightenment leads in turn to knowledge of the One, and consequently to salvation of the soul. Because the various links between the origin of all beings and life on Earth are thought to be tangible in the celestial spheres, they are to a certain extent accessible to the visionary eye.

Mystics of all religions have used the metaphor of the path to describe the different stages and steps leading to God. In Islamic mysticism, the steps along this path represent the different stages reached by the traveler in his ascetic and moral discipline.

Great importance is given to fragrances in these stages. They assist the soul in its journey towards Unity. Special scents are therefore prescribed for each stage of the soul's development, to accompany the searcher through the different stations and assist him on his way.

Amber is the father of all scents and rose the mother; these are the yin and yang of fragrances. When longing for the Divine grows in the soul, the *murid* (literally the "willing," the traveller or searcher) is given amber, rose, jasmine, musk, violet, and incense. They accompany the *murid* at the first station.

The first station (*maqam an-nafs*) is the station of the self or lower soul (*maqam* literally means "station, situation, standing"). Here the searcher learns to master and soften his self and educate his character. His main task is to ready himself. Each human being is born into this station, and most human beings remain there until the end of their lives. When a child is born, it is wholly absorbed in the satisfaction of its physical needs. It wants to be fed, carried and taken care of. Failing that, it will cry, bawl, and shout to achieve its aim as quickly as possible. As a child's body grows, we also expect the soul of a human being to grow and develop beyond the strong egocentrism of childhood. Many people grow physically into adulthood without ever leaving this stage. Such people never stop demanding and remain enslaved by the desire to satisfy the self.

According to the spiritual masters of Islam, this causes many chronic, degenerative, and emotional diseases. This is because the soul, the divine breath, is meant to grow. Such is the meaning of life. When man forgets this (a human being is called *insan* in Arabic, "he who has forgotten") and confines himself to the material world, he damages his soul and thereby harmony on earth. This entanglement in the lower self may be manifested in the form of self-doubt, feelings of oppression, fear, selfishness, depression, suicide, crying fits without any apparent motive, criminal behavior, alcoholism, drug abuse, or sexual perversions.

On the physical plane, this entanglement in the lower level may be manifested by obesity, eye problems, heart attacks, sexual diseases, or cancer. This does not mean, however, that every one of these occurrences should be immediately or solely taken as a manifestation of this first station. Life itself is subject to so many different and intricate circumstances and conditions, that it would be inhuman to draw conclusions from the outside before having touched upon and assimilated all individual nuances. Besides, pleasant and friendly people are found in that station too, since a natural goodness is to be found in each person. Not everyone can or wants to follow the call of the soul.

It is the kindling of the longing to know the Truth that drives a human being to start walking the path towards the One. The methods used to overcome darkness and indolence are self-discipline, patience, compassion, mercy, and responsibility. When one succeeds, one enters the next station, *maqam al-qalb*.

This is the station of the heart. The heart represents the essence of man. It is also the seat of memories and dreams, false hopes and guilt, pebbles of self-interest, wishes, and fears. To empty the "hardened heart," remove the rubble and fill it anew is a major task for every man and woman.

In this phase, the searcher's heart begins to melt and experience all sorts of fluctuations. The searcher feels himself drawn by feelings of love toward all beings; he begins to love others as himself and to see the divine light in them rather than their human weaknesses. The searcher exudes gentleness, calmness, and his eyes fill with tears for no apparent reason. He also becomes moodier; he writhes like a wounded animal, torn apart with anguish. The searcher wanders here and there and runs away, only to return. The metamorphosis has begun.

The scents that accompany the searcher on this station are amber, rose and musk. They mainly help the body overcome the entanglements and illnesses linked to this station. Thus cleansed and detoxified, the body starts to heal itself. This can lead to the following symptoms: skin rash, scalp problems, headaches, especially migraines, fever, diarrhea, nausea, kidney, and gallbladder problems.

In this station, there is no difference between inside and outside and the seeker is cleansed by the divine water of truth.

On the emotional level, ecstasy, joy, depression, anger, arrogance, and intolerance towards other people's feelings may appear. There may also be increased forgetfulness, lack of concentration, fear of failure, and self-deception.

Jasmine, sandalwood, and incense will prove useful in the case of psychological problems.

In this phase, major changes may take place in the searcher's life: separations, friends turning away, financial problems, yet he nevertheless finds himself overcome by a new feeling of joy to be alive.

For in this station, the *murid* wants nothing else but to be with the Divine, to hear the One and see the One in everything. The body is thus purified and a new order comes to be.

The third station (*maqam ar-rooh*) is the station of the soul. From now on, increasing dangers face the searcher, who now needs a teacher to lead the way, a man or a woman who has already traveled the path, faced and overcome its dangers and traps. The outer laws and tasks that are given to the searcher serve to focus all his soul's strength in one direction, so that he may reach happiness. A student is given various exercises to increase his compassion and kindness of heart, and to improve his considerateness, self-examination, and self-discipline. This is the task of the teacher. The soul is helped in its ascension by aloe bark, henna, amber, and musk, while rose and sandalwood are used to assist the searcher on the psychological level.

At this stage, the searcher is perceived as a person of great love and spirituality. Yet even then, he is faced by emotional and mental instability. Faith is always challenged on the way to bliss. Emotional problems appear in the form of arrogance and pride, self-delusion, lack of concentration, vacillations, and sometimes contempt towards others. One who has reached the third station will suffer from those afflictions when he is not yet strong enough to resist the whims of the self.

The following physical disorders may be found in this station: euphoria resulting from excessive breathing exercises, nervous twitches, fatigue, cravings, and fever. Whereas in the first and second stages fever results from the body's cleansing and detoxification, in this stage, it marks the beginning of a deep purification of the soul and the burning of all its impurities.

The fourth station (*maqam as-sirr*) is the stage of mystery, in which the mysteries of the divine laws are revealed to the searcher. He begins to understand the mechanisms that hold the universe together. At this level, he develops full powers of second sight and can read the thoughts of others. At this stage, the searcher no longer pursues selfish aims. He is no longer interested in fame, riches, or any type of sensation. He relates solely to the Divine, to the creator of all things. He remains human nonetheless, and is still affected by physical and emotional events, which can no longer be described as illnesses, but rather as disruptions of balance. These events keep the searcher stuck in this stage, or may even cause him to regress to a lower station, thus preventing him from reaching his goal. The greatest dangers or "disruptions of balance" likely to happen result from misinterpretations of divine phenomena. They include: loss of faith, irrationality, forgetfulness, pain or stinging in the heart region, excessive sensitivity, and lack of interest in life on the physical plane. Useful scents are henna, sandalwood, and aloe bark.

Physical problems which characterize this stage are fever, respiratory disorders, and attacks of asphyxiation resulting from many years of excessive or sometimes erroneous breathing exercises.

Andi Diem

Quietness lies within the whirling...

The link and contacts with the invisible world and its disembodied souls, demons and *djinn*, intensify and may prove troublesome. In such cases, various spiritual practices may be used, including breathing exercises, generally from the Holy Quran, which describes the various breathing forms, beginning, and holding the breath. Some people are able to recite for two minutes straight, spanning four to five octaves, in one single breath.

In the fifth station (*maqam al-fana*, or the "level of dissolution"), the inner nature of human beings—the microcosm—is united with the laws of the

Andi Diem

...consciousness lies in fragrance.

macrocosm, in harmony with the metacosmos, reality and truth. The searcher is then truly capable of seeing the Divine. His or her sight encompasses both this world and the next, the world of other creatures.

Such people find the meaning of life in cultivating and improving their relationship to the Divine. The way to Unity, to the Divine is through dissolution, not through magnification, of the self. At this stage, a searcher deserves the name of human being since he has really become one, and can live as God's servant and representative. He no longer disturbs the harmony of the earth, but acts as a divine instrument preserving this wonderful organism.

On this level, only rose and amber remain to give the soul the last impetus and alleviate any difficulties. However rare, these can be extremely strong, usually taking the form of excessive ecstasy. A human being in such a state is called *majdoob*, completely absorbed in the Divine, the Beloved One, in a permanent state of blissful happiness. Eating or sleeping, clothing or other people's reactions to them do not affect such beings, who live in a totally different reality. Yet this should not be the aim of this station.

At this stage, a searcher may give up speech and remain perfectly silent. Completely engrossed in the music of the universe, he no longer feels any need to communicate. He is plagued by a high degree of forgetfulness:

from one moment to the next, he may forget what he has done or said. The states associated with this stage closely resemble those of the mentally deranged. This is why in the East people who appear insane are treated with great circumspection: they might be blessed by God, and one would come to no good by expressing contempt for them. The higher one gets in the stages of the soul, the greater the danger of being misled by evil forces.

In the sixth station (*maqam al-baqa'*), the searcher reaches the state of *baqa'*, "staying in the Divine," the stage of eternity. What remains is no longer the person the searcher used to be, the person he cherished more than anything on earth before starting on the way to enlightenment. Perfect harmony rules on all levels at this stage, which is beyond all scents, since the soul has finally reached its true goal and found its bliss. Unlike the others, this station cannot be reached through one's own efforts. It is solely for those who have been elected by God. At this stage, a person no longer needs sleep or food. Having overcome all human limitations, he can project himself anywhere. The only physical event that holds him back is death, of which he is forewarned. And death itself is celebrated as a blessing, because such a person has long since given up his connection with the world.

Descriptions and classifications of the various stages vary according to each spiritual school and its teachers, as do the specific states and experiences. This is but an introduction to an extremely complex subject.[41]

The charisma of an enlightened person and the pure being of a child are one and the same. In other words, no matter how many descriptions of the taste, smell, or effect of an apple you may read and study, if you really wish to know what it tastes like, you have to grab the apple and take a bite!

How does all this relate to belly dancing?

With each movement, awareness of the self grows. By experiencing the stillness of pose and movement, the inwardness and ecstasy of the dance, the self loses its boundaries and flows, as perfectly as the power of the ocean is mirrored in each drop of water.

Imagine a room and put your birth at one end of the room, your death at the other. Close your eyes and let your intuition guide you to a place between these two poles that reflects your present stage. Stay there for a while and let yourself be surrounded by your past and your future. Then start shaping the pictures and thoughts that come to you, let them reach your body and let your body lend expression to your mood. Take your time and repeat each movement, each impulse as many times as you wish. Let yourself flow into the past and then again into the future. Where are you, and what does your path look like? Go back to the time of your birth, crouch down and return to that moment when all power was yours and you were surrounded by the scent of paradise.

Dance, again and again, into the future and into the past, until the time comes when you lie down again and the second gate opens, the one called death. Can you smell it? Have you always known, never forgotten? How do you feel?

THE ARMS

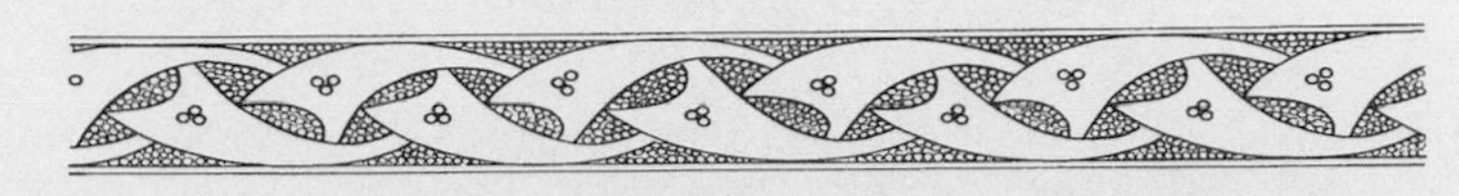

SERPENTS IN THE WIND

From the center, from your belly, your arms reach out to the sky and your legs firmly touch the earth. You are the child of both, and life is mirrored through your being. Dance, sister, dance, for through your dancing life awakens.

When you extend your arms in harmony with your posture and your movement, you can feel them in your belly. Arms and hands play an important part in dancing. Through them you can express pride and sorrow, beckoning and refusal, openness and closure, happiness and shyness.

Open your arms and take in the space around you—above, below, in front, and behind, reach out as far as you can and do not be afraid to become weaker or more vulnerable through this stretching, for your pelvis is always rooted in the center of the earth, and your source lies in yourself. The furthest point always remains an expression of the innermost.

Snake Arms

This movement starts from the shoulders, with the palms of your hand facing down. This is followed by a flowing movement, as if the arms were boneless. The ensuing intensive shoulder massage dissolves all tensions gradually.

Start by opening your chest and remaining open so that your shoulders can enjoy the greatest possible freedom of movement. Then start by raising your arms laterally along your body, first the right arm, then the left, and let your arms gently find their rhythm, like a windmill in the wind. Your hands flow in accordance with the rotating movement. The great secret of snake arms lies in the ability to let go. You become overwhelmed by the feeling that you are diving into the flow of life and coming up again as the bearer of wisdom. The movement flows from the shoulders, through the arms and to the hands,

Andi Diem

Open your arms when you dance, my daughter, for through your dancing life will awaken.

until the lungs fill with air and cleanse themselves. The whole body becomes energized. This is the meaning of snake arms.

The Loop of Infinity (see The Hips, p 104)
When the hips rise and fall in a figure eight, or loop of infinity, the arms almost automatically follow them. Place your arms at the back, at hip level, palms uppermost. Bring your hands towards your belly until the backs of your hands are touching, and open them like a flower, palms up, a hollow space that can give and take, a gesture where giver and beggar meet. Don't let your hands linger, but take them behind your back, along your hips. Make a little circle

Andi Diem

My child, how often I lovingly open my arms to you.

with your knuckles and bring your hands back to the starting position. The coming and going of the arms and hands symbolizes the endless movement of life. Birth and death are the impulse of each movement.

The Arms and the Hip Shimmy (see The Pelvis, p 110)
When your pelvis is swinging and all the pores in your body are opening, stretch your arms horizontally, turn the palm of your left hand toward the earth and the palm of your right hand toward the sky. During the shimmy, bring your arms slowly and calmly up until they meet above your head and your palms are joined, then separate them and bring them back into the position of duality.

The left arm with the palm turned down symbolizes a woman's link to the earth, to nature, and to the material world.

The right arm with the palm turned up stands for a woman's spiritual side. It is precisely through her connection to life, through her affirmation of life, that a woman's spirituality, sensitivity, and nostalgia for unity are born.

By connecting both sides, making the arms meet and the palms join in the form of a tent, the dancer reaches unity and experiences the link between both worlds.

The Tent

The tent symbolizes unity. It builds a protection born out of the dancing woman herself, out of her own inner strength and balance. In the tent, both palms are touching. A variation consists of crossing the wrists so that the hands are entwined; breathing is deepened by the raised rib cage.

Raised and Extended Arm Position (see The Hips, pp 104-109)

This position of the arms can be used in all movements, in particular in the hip drops and lifts. One arm is stretched upwards, while the other is extended horizontally and laterally. This is to help the balance and steady the feet. The hands form a relaxed extension of the arms. In the hip drop and lift, the arm opposite the extended leg is stretched upwards. This helps you to stay in your center. You hold on to the sky with one arm while resting on the earth with the other.

Separation Movement

Extend both arms in front of you, at shoulder level. The back of your right hand is turned to the sky, the back of your left hand to the earth, so that you can see your left palm. Simultaneously lower your right arm and raise your left arm. When you reach the end of the movement, switch the positions of the hands so that you now see your right palm and the back of your left hand. Keep moving your arms up and down, as if you were building a wall of energy between yourself and your surroundings, behind which you can choose to show yourself or remain hidden. Practice this exercise until you can feel it flow, and you become aware of the energy thus created. This is a relaxed and enjoyable way to practice separating from the outside world and being with yourself. When the understanding that there is no difference between the outer and inner world fills your body, then you have understood the movement.

THE HANDS

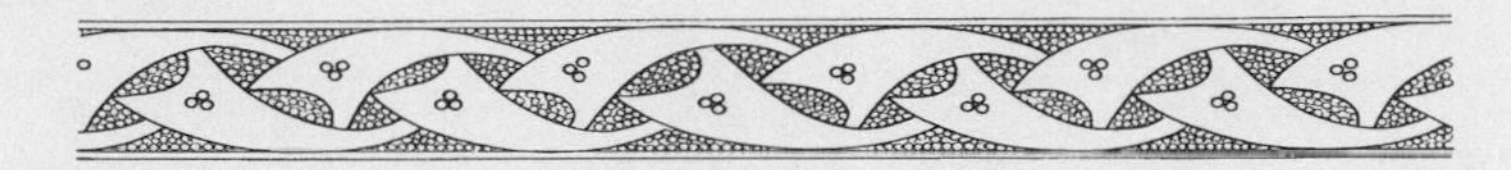

GIVING IS THE SOURCE OF RECEIVING

The first contact we make with another human being takes place through the hand. When two palms meet, a part of the body rich in sensory nerve endings comes into contact with another. A whole world of information is transmitted through this part of the body.

In the East, it is very important for the palm to be kept soft and supple, by means of henna coloring. Henna protects the palms against the weather and shields their many sensory nerves. It is customary for the whole palm to be painted or adorned with henna, all the way to the sensitive fingertips.

Hands also reveal the slightest physical stress. Excessive strain as well as age show themselves in the way the hands are held.

Exercise in Giving

Give someone you like a massage. If you wish to use oil or lotion, warm it in your hands before you start the massage. Keep your movements strong, yet gentle, full, and flowing into one another. Always go back to the end of your last movement before starting the next one, so that you don't startle the person you are massaging. The skin is the organ that connects us to the world. As the one giving the touch, you become the world's most intensely felt messenger. Give as you would like to receive, so that the one who touches and the one who is touched may become one, the giving and the receiving inseparable and reversible at any moment.

Finger Positions in Belly Dancing

This tip will enable you to hold your fingers gracefully from the beginning. Hold your index finger slightly raised, and let the other fingers simply drop in a relaxed manner. In this way, your whole concentration will be in your forefinger and thumb. Concentrate all your energy in the forefinger, which becomes the furthermost point of the arm. This finger position is also used in prayers because it indicates unity. This is why the index finger is called the "witness finger" in Arabic.

When you dance, put all the riches of your inner life, all your experiences,

Holzknecht

Soft yet strong, purposeful yet quick,
the hands glide into the dancing.

all your knowledge, and all your pride into your hands, and let your strength shine out into the world.

Basic Posture

In the basic posture, the palms of the hands face the sky at hip level, like shells. You can return to this position whenever you practice a new movement that you are not ready to accompany with hands and arms.

Wrist Circles

Adopt the finger position described above, and start circling your hand from the wrist down, the lower arm merely following in a reflex movement. You can intensify the movement by bending and stretching your fingers. This bending and stretching is described as giving and taking, where taking is the source of giving, and both are related. Of course, you can practice giving and taking without circling the hands. This is the most frequently used hand movement in the dance, and it is meant to express the idea that no human being is excluded from the circle and that we are all linked in a never-ending story.

UNRWA

The hollow of the hand, shown in the act of both giving and receiving, is the same for teacher and pupil.

In some places in Africa, a gift received is paid back by making another gift, not necessarily to the person who gave you one, since what matters is the giving, and that the flow of giving and taking not be interrupted.

Give free rein to your imagination, and find your own movements with the "movement of giving and taking" and the wrist circles.

Holding the Back of the Hands Against the Forehead (See Sun Circle, p 113)
In the sun circle, the lower abdomen bends and stretches to the limit, so as to form the largest possible circle. You build your own big sun, using your arms

and hands to keep you in your center. The left arm is stretched out, while you rest the back of your right hand on your forehead. In this manner, you practice staying in your center during extreme movements.

We are said to spend most of our lives asleep. We are awake, yet asleep, unaware of ourselves. Here is a little trick to train your wakefulness: press your forefinger and thumb together, as strongly as possible, then pursue your other activities. As long as your fingers are firmly pressed together, you are alert. After a while—at first, maybe after a few minutes—the pressure will unconsciously lessen, and your "being here and now" will fade away. Nevertheless, the longer you practice, the shorter the intervals between being awake and being asleep will become. Body and mind are very clever; they will try to trick you to return to their usual comfortable state. The body will help you press the finger muscles without maintaining the desired degree of wakefulness. Whenever you become aware of this, you will need to think up another tension exercise, for instance by moving the wakeful tension to the arm muscle.

Wakefulness starts with observing yourself, which in turn leads to understanding yourself.

THE BREAST

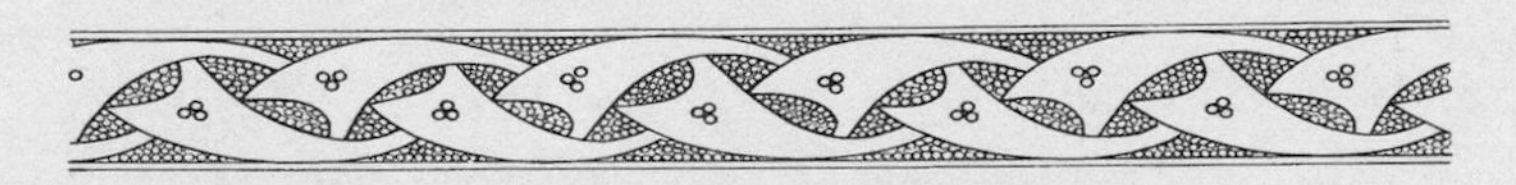

THE BREATH OF DIVINITY LIES IN YOUR BREAST

The breast and chest are the symbol of giving, nourishment, bodily warmth, compassion, and love. They are the clearest expression of giving to the outside. Here a child receives this world's first nourishment; here the most intimate link between a mother and her child is formed.

According to an old Arab tradition, whenever a praying woman has a fervent request, she bares her right breast and speaks out. Calling on divine mercy, she says, "By my right breast and my sad heart, I beg for...!" An Arabic proverb says, "Men know no compassion, for their breasts have no milk!"

Once, when a Bedouin woman wanted to adopt a child, she would lay it against her breast and utter the following words: "Now you are my child in

God's book, for you have suckled at my breast, like all the children I have begotten." The same gesture was made to adopt an adult.

According to Islamic law, children breastfed by the same woman are siblings and marriage between them is as taboo as between blood siblings.

Breathing plays a particularly important part in all the following movements. The lungs are the only inner organ that can be controlled by the will. All the other bodily functions escape our consciousness. Voluntary control of the lungs during inhalation and exhalation can be extended to influence the other organs. Awareness of the organic connection between the individual organs increases through the rhythm of the body and the breathing, which are intimately linked. All tensions and psychological states are mirrored in your breathing. For instance, fear makes you hold your breath, which leads to sudden disruption in the regions of the heart and diaphragm. You might feel as if your heart had stopped, or as if the area just below the breastbone had suddenly gone cold. By restoring space to the extensor muscles, deep breathing and leaning back can help you release yourself from the tense, tight state of fear. This is how a human being can regain his inner balance through breathing exercises.

The chest contains two major organs: the lungs and the heart. By controlling breathing, we can calm our spirit, open, and soothe our heart and solar plexus.

Anatomically speaking, the right lung is divided into three segments, while the left lung only has two larger lobes. Both lungs are activated by three different muscle groups.

Exercises

The following exercises stimulate all segments:

The upper part of the lungs is activated by the neck muscles. Take the basic position and balance your weight on both legs. Rest your chin on your breast. Now move your head once to the right and then to the left, in a sliding motion.

The middle part of the lungs is activated by the large thoracic muscle, that is by moving the rib cage to the right and then to the left.

The lower part of the lungs is activated by the diaphragm, namely by contracting and relaxing the muscle of the diaphragm. With time, this movement becomes so fast and relaxed that the whole chest starts vibrating, or rather fluttering.

These movements are all part of belly dancing, which demonstrates the underlying wisdom of this ancient dance form.

The following movement activates the three groups of muscles related to your lungs, thus lengthening and deepening your breath:

Take up the basic position. Fold your hands in front of you at the level of your lower abdomen. Now raise your folded hands over your head and let them slowly slide behind your head, down to the upper part of your back.

Trust is the mother of opening.

Andi Diem

Now press your hands together and push them downwards against your back. Bring them slowly back to the starting position.[42] Repeat three times. If you begin a new day with this exercise, it will have a cleansing and stimulating effect on your whole body.

The chest and the arms form a whole: without the collarbone and the shoulder blades, which are linked to the chest, we cannot move the arms. This is why, in all the following exercises, it is advisable to extend the arms at shoulder level and keep the hands as far apart as possible.

When you dance, when your pelvis is flying and your belly vibrating, when your upper thigh is shaking and your diaphragm fluttering, forget about breathing in: it will happen naturally, in answer to your breathing out. Exhale fully, make yourself empty, and inhaling will follow of its own accord and fill you up.

At my breast you grow into a human being.

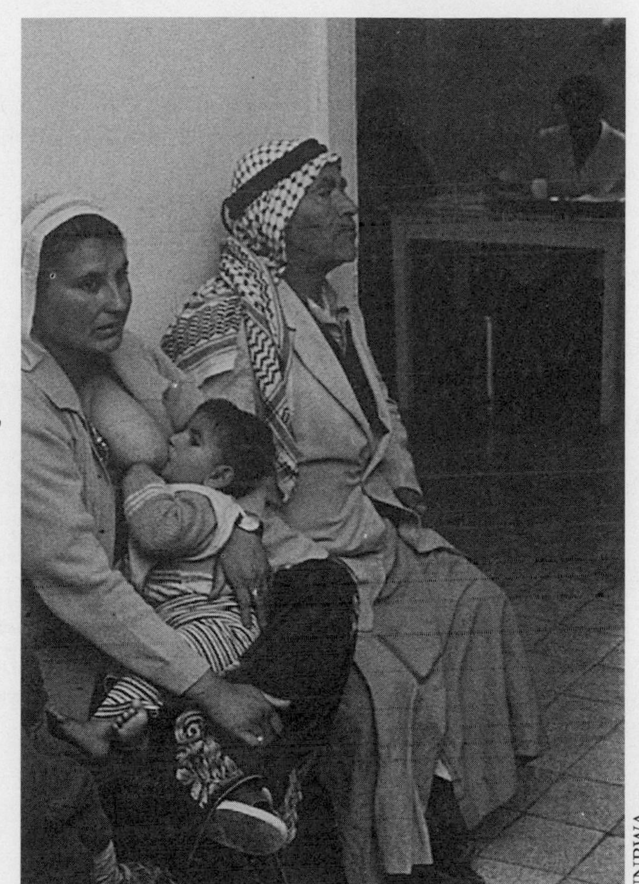

UNRWA

Rib Cage Slides

Take up the basic position. Balance your weight on both legs. Take a deep breath and lift your rib cage. Slide it slowly to the left, breathe out and let it drop. Then breathe in, lift your rib cage and return to the middle, breathe out and let it drop. While you are still in the middle, lift your rib cage again by taking a deep breath, and slide to the right. Then come back to the middle as before. You have just completed a full cycle.

In this movement, shoulders and hips face the front, the rib cage moving independently from them.

This movement is particularly relaxing during pregnancy, when the baby's head puts pressure on the diaphragm. It should only be practiced up to the seventh month, however, since by then the baby is too big to leave enough space in the mother's belly for such movements.

Rib Cage Circles (Horizontal)
For this exercise, picture four dots on an imaginary circle drawn around you: front left, front right, back right and back left. Take up the basic position in the middle. Use the same technique as before by lifting your rib cage through a deep inhalation, but this time slide it to the front and left, breathe out, then breathe in and slide to the front and right, then breathe out. Lift your rib cage again and slide it towards the back and right, and breathe out. Inhale again and slide your rib cage to the left and back, then breathe out. Inhale again and slide it to the front and left, then breathe out. Slide back into your center.

Rib Cage Circle (Vertical)
The easiest way to make this wave is by visualizing a dial, and following it with your chest. Put the ball of your thumbs on your hipbones, and bend your knees slightly. Start by taking a deep breath and sliding your rib cage towards twelve o'clock, then slide to one, two, three and so on, until you come back to twelve o'clock, then return to the basic position.

All these rib cage movements contribute greatly to the flexibility of the upper body and awaken the body's intelligence. Physical control is improved, and you will discover parts of your body and muscles that you were probably never aware of before.

THE SHOULDERS

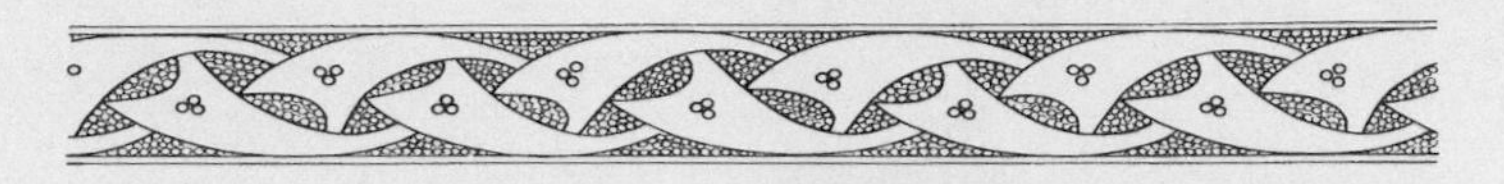

MEEKNESS RESTS PROUDLY ON YOUR SHOULDERS

Moods are revealed most clearly by our shoulders. When we are sad or depressed, our shoulders droop, and when we feel good they automatically open and our chest is filled with joy. In Arabic we speak of people "carrying worries on their shoulders." Any pressure shows in the way we hold our shoulders. This is why it is important to become aware of them and strengthen them. Our body reads our feelings more accurately than our mind; as we strengthen our body, we become better at coping with our moods and the opportunities to come closer to our self multiply.

Close your eyes, anchor your feet into the ground and turn your gaze inwards. Put your thumbs in your navel, the palms and the other fingers resting on your belly. Take a deep breath and let it fill your belly so that it becomes a round vessel holding all your feelings, all your thoughts.

Let your belly become the earth out of which a plant can grow, nourished by your awareness, and let the plant grow over your breast, all the way to your shoulders.

The inner plant grows strong, green and full of vitality, it sprouts and joyfully turns each of your shoulders into a flower, as beautiful and colorful as only you can make it. Your shoulders have now blossomed into two open flowers.

Shoulder Roll

Close your eyes for a while and relax. Balance your weight on both legs. Focus on your shoulders and let your inner eye touch them. Now concentrate on your right shoulder. Keep your eyes closed and slowly raise your shoulder upwards a little, pull it towards the back and let it come back to the starting position. Do this slowly and carefully. Put all your being into this movement.

Intensify this movement yet again, by bringing your shoulders further back. Imagine three stages: front, in the middle, behind. Behind and then back to the starting position.

The sequence is as follows: raise your shoulders, bring them to the back, let them fall, raise them again, take them further back and let them fall,

Holzknecht

Relaxation is the name of the shoulders in dancing...

and a third time. Then repeat the movement but this time to the front. You can either practice with a partner or alone, in front of a mirror, to observe yourself.

Shoulder Circles
The shoulder circle intensifies the previous movement. Arch your shoulders as far back as possible. Let them fall into the starting position. Make sure that your chest remains open, your neck relaxed and that the movement is confined to your shoulders.

Andi Diem

...and confidence the name of the shoulders for the child.

Now shift your weight to your left leg, lean your upper body slightly towards the back and extend the right leg forward so that your whole body is aligned. In this position, your upper body is given the maximum free space for your shoulders to open up during the movement.

These two exercises are particularly enjoyable when you use them to seduce. Find a partner or stand in front of a mirror and use your shoulders to charm your partner—or yourself—out of her—or your—reserve. Slightly lower your head and look at your intended "victim" with heartbreaking eyes.

Put all of your strength, all of yourself into that look and seduce with your shoulders, irresistibly.

Shoulder Shimmy

Put yourself in the basic position, bend your knees and bring your hands level with your hips. Move alternate shoulders to the front and to the back. Keep the oscillation small, never more than a few centimetres. Gradually, increase the speed until the movement becomes a flutter, a vibration. Women often find the shoulder shimmy (isolated shoulder shake) quite difficult. Yet the most important thing is to let go, abandon yourself to the fast rhythm of the music, relax, and not create any performance stress. So take your time, all the time you need, and don't put pressure on yourself or get the wrong idea. The shoulder shimmy is one of the healthiest movements in belly dancing: the meridian of the small intestine flows between the shoulder blades, which are themselves linked to the ovaries. When you bring the upper body to a vibrating point, your muscles relax, your body becomes warm, and coldness and rigidity are transformed into warmth and vitality.

Fears, identity crises, and emotional problems are either located in the shoulders or in the lower belly, where they usually correspond to fears of a sexual nature. When you practice the shoulder shimmy, you pluck up the strength and courage to turn these fears into joy and zest for life. Your lips soften, a smile shines on your face: "I'm here, I'm alive, I feel young and full of strength. I trust in myself and I'm shimmering with *joie de vivre*!" Such is the meaning of the shoulder shimmy.

THE HIPS

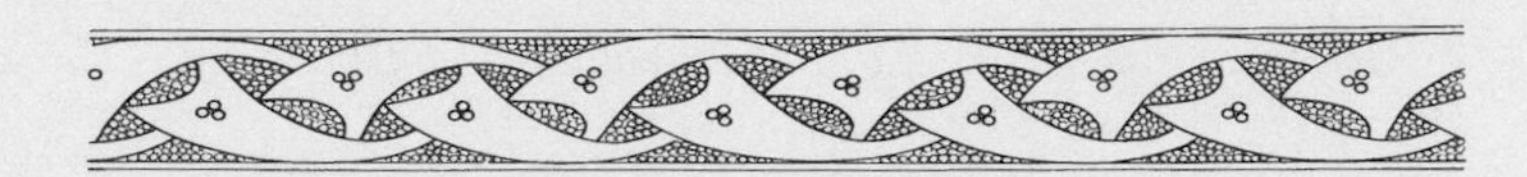

WHEN YOUR HIPS CIRCLE, THE WHOLE UNIVERSE SWINGS ALONG

The hips are two shell-shaped walls that contain the pelvis. How soft and supple they become with this dance! Hip movements require less effort than other belly dancing movements. The important thing is to keep your knees bent, your head high and your chest open to leave enough space for the heart.

Hip Swing

Shift your weight on to your left leg and place your right leg in front of you, balanced on the ball of the foot. The hip has now enough space to move freely. Throw your right hip upwards, while keeping the ball of your foot on the ground and your upper body still. Repeat the movement a few times, then change and try with the left hip. The strength of the swing comes from the hip alone! The whole lower belly is projected sideways and to the front. When you get the feeling that you can make this movement effortlessly—without tensing your shoulders or your neck and without blocking your breath—then you're doing it right. You swing your hip outwards and yet you sit in yourself. You send your energy from your hips into the space around you; it travels from your hips and fills the space with your strength, your inner impulse, invisible yet perceptible. You give your strength a shape, a face. You swirl up everything around you and absorb it.

You can also perform the hip swing while turning around yourself. In that case, your front foot is used as a compass. Your arms are held up and to the side.

Hip Drop

In contrast to the hip swing, in which the movement is directed upwards, the hip drop is a downward movement. You perform it as if you wanted to sit on an invisible chair, changed your mind at the last minute and stood up again. You bend your knees and lower your body, but all the time you sit in yourself, drawing your security and your strength from inside. No matter how far down you go, you never forget who you are. Your forehead is relaxed in the knowledge that meekness is the sister of pride.

Hip Sway

Imagine a child sitting on your right hip. Now move him to your left hip. Practice until you feel that the child could fall asleep, until the movement turns into a wave, until the wave carries you away and *you* become the baby.

Hip Thrust

Take the basic position. Center yourself. Now bring your right hip bone forward; your left hip bone will automatically go backwards. Alternate bringing right and left hip bones forward, as if trying to throw a ball with each forward thrust. Between each movement, take time to pause in the middle, like so: left hip bone forward, basic position, right hip bone forward, basic position, and so on. Let all your strength and self-confidence come to the fore in this movement! The wilder your thrust, the quieter and more sober you'll feel inside yourself.

Holzknecht

The whole space around you is swung on the strength of your hips...

Andi Diem

...the child sits securely on your hip.

Let all the tensions, the laws and disciplining—whether imposed by the outside or by yourself—flow out and let yourself be swept away in the intense moment of dancing.

If you thrust your right and left hips in a forward diagonal direction, at a crazily fast rhythm, you'll progress to the hip shimmy.

Hip Shimmy

As always in belly dancing, one muscle group is isolated; in the hip shimmy, it is the lower back and buttocks. Above the waist, the body remains motionless, while the muscles of that area twitch. An experienced dancer will shake her whole trunk in the hip shimmy. As described earlier on, the hip shimmy may either result from an alternate hip thrust or from an alternate forward-backward vibration of the knees. You can do it! Sometimes it takes but an instant, sometimes a little longer. Listen to the drum, pick up the vibrations and let go. Give in to the urge of your muscles and shout with delight!

And what about the arms? The arms move softly, snake-like, to a totally different rhythm. The head rests majestically, the eyes sparkle, the lips are soft, the jaws, and the shoulders quietly relaxed.

What is the meaning of this distribution of the body into different movements in space and time? The different speeds with which the body plays, the different centers with which you dance, alternating and together, exhaust your rational train of thoughts, leaving space for inner impulses, for the strength that stems from the belly. Reason becomes blurred and the wild woman wins. The many and the various become one; individual parts melt into a whole. The fears which have set into your hips, your belly and your buttocks melt in the fire of your joy to be alive and change into happiness and wild energy. Your spine becomes supple and the individual vertebrae find their true place. Such is the meaning of the hip shimmy.

Figure Eight, or Loop of Infinity

Picture a figure eight on the floor. Place yourself exactly in its center, your right foot in one loop, your left foot in the other. Now let your hips follow the loop. Pull your right hip to the back (by doing so your left hip will automatically come forward) and follow the loop. When you reach the crossing of the loops, let the right hip pick up the movement by pushing it backwards and following the loop with a forward movement.

The figure eight illustrates the deep philosophy that underlies belly dancing. An eight contains both the line and the circle. A straight line between two dots, on which you can advance and retreat, purposeful and direct, into the future and back into the past. And the circle, without beginning or end, self-contained, perfect, and alone.

Walk along a straight line; at the end of the line, before you reach the wall, turn on your axis and describe a full left turn and walk towards the other wall in a diagonal. When you reach the wall, turn on your axis and describe a full right turn so that you walk once more diagonally to the other wall. By turning on your own axis, you have united both forms of line and circle.

The circle and the straight line are given forms, but the figure eight, this symbol of infinity, is yours. It is through uniting both inside and outside that you reach infinity and awareness is born.[43] Observe the movements of your arms and hands (see p 89) that complete this figure. Your arm movements illustrate this finite world while your pelvis describes infinity. Through these movements you shape the worlds in which people show themselves and you experience the philosophy that says: "Live and act on earth, in this world, as if you were to live forever; live and prepare yourself for the next world, as if you were to say goodbye any time." Through the figure eight, the symbol of infinity, you overcome the seemingly insurmountable walls that separate both worlds and you come closer to the essential.

The figure eight has many faces. You can make it flat and narrow, high and round, you can perform it with bent or straight knees. In the latter position you'll let your heels rise up to accompany each loop. The choice is yours, and so is the mood that you wish to express.

Figure Eight with a Double Circle

Again, picture a figure eight on the floor, yet this time add two circles to the middle crossing. Start moving to the right with your right hip and make the outer circle by bringing it from the back forward, along the outer circle, then make the front circle and take the movement over to the left hip by pushing it forward and continuing the outer circle, making a second circle when you come to the back. Now take the movement over to your right hip, and so on. Both inner circles make a figure eight that consists of two distinct circles, apparently unconnected in space. This wild movement requires the whole volume of your body to become full and earthy. It needs a strong connection to the earth through the feet and a deep, primeval laugh, to really succeed. The Great Mother is dancing...

It sounds more difficult than it is in reality. Try it first in your thoughts, then let your hips take the lead. Not only is this movement great fun, it is also particularly good for all tensions in the sacrum area (especially at the time of menstruation) and for headaches. This is because all the reflex zones located on both sides of the spine and relating to the urinary bladder, kidneys, small intestine, spleen, heart, and lungs are stimulated and the hips as well as the pelvis can play with the whole range of movements.

THE PELVIS

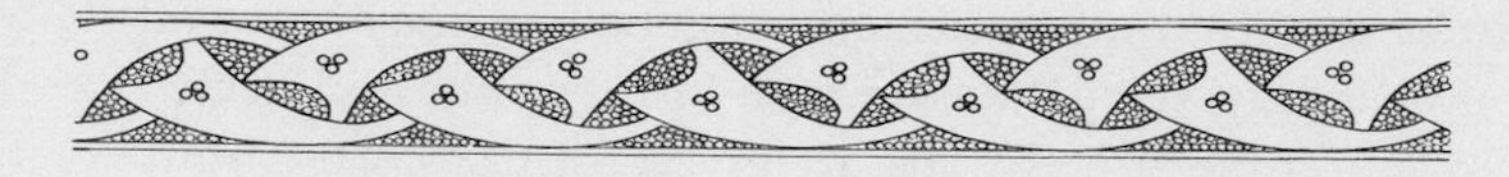

THE SNAKE OF SPONTANEITY IS COILED IN THE PELVIS

The spine is supported by the pelvis. On top of the spine sits the head. All other parts of the trunk either hang from the spine or from the ribs, which themselves hang from the spine. The pelvis actually supports the whole body. The freer, the looser the movements of your pelvis, the better you can control your pelvic joints, and the greater the strength and spontaneity of your entire body. To let the pelvis go, to shake the hips, touches on deeply seated sexual taboos. Yet the pelvis makes no distinction between permissible or prohibited movements. The pelvis only knows stiffness or flexibility. Your pelvis is potentially a source of deep feelings and great strength. More than that, since the whole pelvic area is the basis of all movements, it constitutes the real foundation of life. The pelvis holds the genitals; it must be free from constraints and rigidity; it must literally be free to move in all directions and circle around the gravity center of the body, like a ball around its middle.[44] This is because the center of this ball is the focal point of all actions. Forcing the pelvis into a fixed position, restricting its mobility, whether as a result of cultural taboos or emotional blockages, results in rigidity in the small of the back and therefore a stiffening of the place in the body where all stresses and tensions meet.

Our physical tensions reflect our inner tensions. Their roots may be found in repressed feelings and unsolved conflicts. There is no physical exercise which can solve the cause of such conflicts or neuroses. Yet the movements can help you become aware of the tensions in your body and break away from the never ending circle of thoughts. That alone is a major step. When you examine the things in yourself that are stiff, those things that won't be budged, everything inside you that say "No," then your feelings can start flowing and your body can loosen itself. This is the beginning of the healing process.

In belly dancing, the drum is the sister of the pelvis. It is through the beating drum that the pelvis is called out of its reserve. As the drum beats on, the pelvis is set in motion and the rest of the body flies away on the inspired wings of the melody.

Take the time to observe yourself in your daily activities: when you write, when you cook, when you wash, when you type, when you vacuum, or when you're tidying up. When you get the feeling that your face is tense, when your eyes feel heavy, when your eyebrows frown, when your shoulders hurt, your jaws tighten up, and your teeth clench, then circle with your pelvis, find your center in your pelvis and balance on it. A smile will soon play on your lips, your breathing will find its own rhythm, your facial muscles relax and your shoulders resume their proper task. Remember to visualize that the movements must be carried by those muscles which can move your buttocks, for these are the strongest muscles in your body.

Whenever you feel that a movement is easy, it means that it is performed in the adequate proportion. So play with your pelvis, give it a chance to make you light-footed, to help you. Use it, experiment with it. You can change your whole life by drawing on your pelvis. Spontaneity, joy of life, self-confidence, a more intense love life, and a greater circle of friends can all be the outcome. Try it!

There are many variations on the pelvic circle in belly dancing. The circle is the most perfect movement. The great circle knows no beginning or end, no nostalgia, no separation; it is all-encompassing, all-receiving, and stands for the Great Mother. The great ball of the earth is reflected in you when you circle your pelvis. Your strength is coiled up, strong and quiet in your navel. Then comes an impulse, a vibration, and the pelvis gives in and starts circling, slowly, shaping the round, full strength into a circle, circling quietly and carefully at first, like intuition being born. Then a deep breathing gains your hips and the circle grows, becomes more confident and daring, and the nostalgia awakens. The source of all your strength grows over and beyond the limits of your body. Your skin becomes more porous and you take in all the space around you. It pushes you further, beyond the room; your hips circle and take in all your surroundings, the trees, the houses, the streets, over and away from the city, over the mountains, the fields, the forests, all the way to the rivers and the oceans. Your lips are salty and you stretch over the steppes and the deserts, over the whole great ball, further and further into the stars, into the whole, into the universe. Limitless, endless...

Again, the impulse calls you back. Slowly the circle, that source of strength, contracts and returns from the wide spaces back into the intensity of the center, over the landscapes, the mountains, the city, back into the room where you're standing, into your body, your belly, into the concentrated dot of your navel. And this is where your thumbs are resting, your hands hanging loosely below.

The Moon Circle

Take the basic position. Let your hips make a small, full circle. The movement

Andi Diem

Full is the pelvis, strong the stance in the flow of dancing.

does not come from the legs, but from the pelvis. It is activated by muscles in the buttocks and the upper thighs. Take your time to perform this movement, for it is the basis, the essence. Through the moon circle, you will always be able to relax your hips and your pelvis and center yourself. The hip circle is a slow descent into yourself.

You can either hold your arms in the basic position or open them up as if to hug a huge tree trunk.

UNRWA

Full is my pelvis, quiet the walk in the flow of time.

Shooting Stars on the Moon Circle

Again, circle your hips, but this time lift and drop your pelvis as you circle, as if you were dropping dots on your circle. You are then performing two movements at the same time.

The Sun Circle

In this circle, you let your pelvis draw the biggest circle, and in order to do so, you push your pelvis forward, while bending your upper body backwards . If you bring the back of your left hand to your forehead while extending the right arm sideways, it will help make a big circle while remaining centered (see The Arms, p 89).

The Double Circle

Imagine two separate circles, of identical size, one next to the other, and follow them with your pelvis. Start with the circle on your right: put your weight on your right leg and let your pelvis circle counter-clockwise. Once you have reached the middle, shift your weight to the left leg and make another circle, counter-clockwise too.

The Pelvis Shimmy

In the pelvis shimmy, we spread the feet further apart than usual, bending slightly deeper into the knees. This is more taxing on the upper thighs and it is a good idea to shake the legs every so often to prevent any tension in the upper thigh muscles. The muscles of the buttocks take the pelvis forward and backward while the belly remains totally relaxed, loose, and soft. This is an archaic movement in which it is essential that you sit in yourself. Imagine a straight, clear ray of light shining from above, through your head, along your trunk, between your legs, into the ground. Open your shoulders, hold your head high and do the shimmy! With time, you'll find this movement so easy that you'll get your pelvis into a gallop. You will feel your pelvis becoming looser and your lower body opening in release. Your vagina and anus relax and even your jaws become soft.

THE BELLY

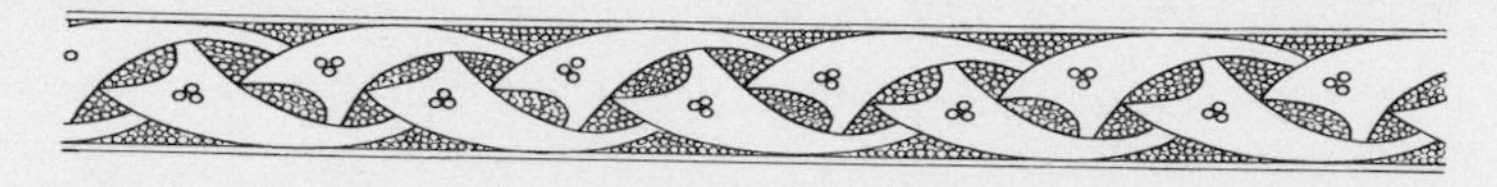

AS FULL AS THE MOON, AS SOFT AS CLOUDS IN THE WIND

No other parts of the body have fallen prey to so many half truths as the belly and the lower abdomen. According to some, the belly should be flat and hard as a plank; others would have it constantly pulled in.

Others yet maintain that the belly should be kept soft and free of all constraints.

Really, none of these extremes is correct. Just as do the heart, lungs, voice box, and their supporting muscles, the lower abdomen hangs on the spine. It follows that when the spine and head are in the correct position, the floor of the pelvis, diaphragm, throat, and tongue are given the proper tension. The contents of the lower abdomen—that is to say, everything below the diaphragm—do not require any deliberate tension. Indeed, when the position is right (which is only possible when all parts can move freely) there is no need for any deliberate tension, which would indeed only disturb the natural measure of contraction.

What happens when the abdomen contracts?

The upper part of the pelvis is tilted backwards, the pelvis loses its flexibility and the small of the back is under excessive strain, because the pelvis cannot carry the spine as it should. The flow of movements becomes irregular, the shoulders stressed and tense. When, in addition, the abdomen is pulled upwards, the lower ribs stick out too much, the chest stiffens, breathing becomes shallow and the neck tenses up. It would be a shame to restrict one's spontaneity and charm and accept all these tensions, only to answer the demands of social ideals that currently advocate a flat belly.

What does matter is to strengthen the muscles of the pelvic floor, which plays a major part in supporting the abdomen and its weighty contents. These muscles can be strengthened every day without spending much time, whenever one goes to the toilet.

Try holding the urine flow and then letting go. Then try to make the flow very strong. In other words, do not let the flow just be, but use this exercise to get it under control. This is the easiest way to strengthen the perineum. This is important after pregnancy, when these muscles have been particularly strained.

Elderly women often complain that they keep losing a few drops of urine and have to wear sanitary pads; if you exercise these muscles, this will not happen. Once you have "discovered" your perineum, you can train it whenever you wish, while waiting at the bus stop, during a long car drive, at the office, or while you're cooking. No one will see that you're exercising!

When you perform belly dancing, you can always involve the perineum. Observe how pulling this muscle affects your movements.

If you strengthen your perineum, in time you will come to realize that a circle of energy is closing, which extends from your head along your trunk all the way to the perineum and upwards along the spine—like a egg of light. It may be that, unbeknownst to you, this energy has so far leaked out. Helping yourself to this energy and strengthening it can refine your body awareness and give you a feeling for what happens inside. This leads to self-confidence, feeling centered, an alert and calm look, with relaxed, powerful arms and hands.

Holzknecht

The belly is the drum of femininity in dancing...

Belly Wave

In the belly wave, the dancer imitates the belly's contractions during labor. The whole lower abdomen, starting from the diaphragm, is massaged and stimulated through this movement. The contractions of the belly lead you to a deep, gentle trance, which relaxes and sensitizes the whole body. The inner organs are massaged and stimulated through the isolated movements of the upper and lower belly muscles. This in turn leads to a feeling of global well-being. Masked sexual anxieties reach the conscious level and can find a solution. The belly wave can be performed in two directions. Choose the one which feels most comfortable.

Margreth Nowinski

...and in life.

First Variation

Take the basic position. Both thumbs rest on your navel; your hands lie on your lower belly. Push your lower belly outwards. Then pull your lower belly in and up, all the way to your diaphragm and pull in your diaphragm too. Now push your diaphragm out and let it roll down. Your lower belly rolls outwards. Repeat.

Second Variation

Take the basic position. Take a deep breath. Push out only your diaphragm and let it roll downwards, and push your lower belly out. Then pull your lower belly in as much as you can and again push your diaphragm out, and so on.

Once you master the belly wave in the standing position, practice it while walking or lying down.

The belly wave is at its most intense when performed in a circle with other women. The music used for this movement is dominated by drums, since it is the drums that have the most direct effect on consciousness. Each beating of the drum is picked up as an impulse by the belly. The belly becomes an expression of yourself with each wave.

The belly wave can lead to a gentle, deep meditation.

Belly Flutter

The diaphragm is at the center of this movement. In the beginning, you can make this movement easier in two different ways: you can either keep your mouth open and pant or else hold your breath. Contract your diaphragm and then push it out. Start with a slow movement, then increase the speed until the movement becomes a vibration, a fluttering.

To find your diaphragm, the best way is to relax your belly and then produce a sound coming from deep inside you, something like "ah!" or "ha!" When you shout, you push air out of your lungs, which results automatically in a strong contraction of the diaphragm. Exercise until you can use this muscle at will.

THE LEGS

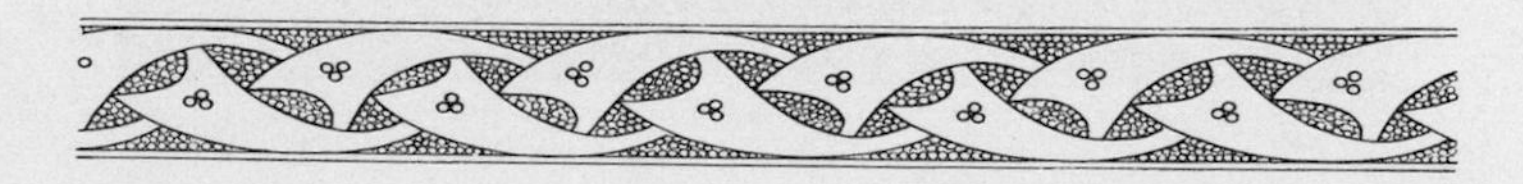

THE PILLARS OF THE TEMPLE

I want strong, sturdy legs to carry me through the hills and valleys

Most of us are not happy with our legs, which we find either too short, too thick or too thin.

In reality, the beauty of the legs has much more to do with their agility and their mobility than with their visual shape. The knee joints control the movements of the lower leg, or follow when the weight of the hips has an effect on them from the top down. The softer the hip joints, the richer the variations of the knee movements and the more beautiful the shape of the legs.

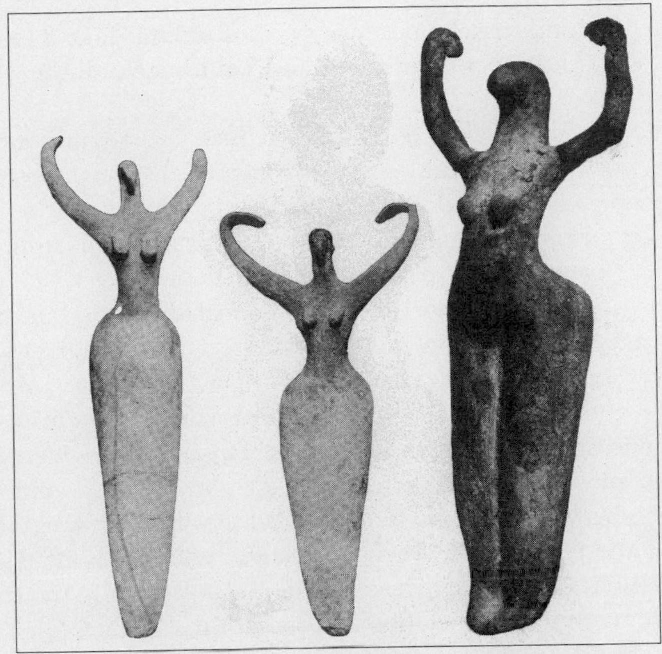

Newman 1974, Bildteil, S.26

The pillars of the dancer...

...and of the temple.

Sit on the floor and stretch your legs in front of you. Take a look at them, letting your eyes glide over your calves and your knees, all the way to your thighs.

Look at all the so-called "defects" that disturb you about your legs—the weak connective tissue, the undesired split capillaries or varicose veins, the unwanted shapes, and the cellulite.

Let your gaze brush softly and quietly over your legs and let them tell you your story. For each of these pictures, like the expressive wrinkles of your face, carries in itself your experiences, your personal life story, your soul. Accept what seems ugly to you as something meaningful and do not let yourself be devastated by common beauty standards.

Bring your legs to your breast and hug them as you would a beloved human being. Love and attention are two things that can carry the whole world.

Through belly dancing and its movements, you can give your legs, your calves and thighs, your knee and foot joints all the attention that they need to become firm and strong. Your thighs especially will finally receive through the pelvic play of belly dancing the exercise that suits them. And there is one thing you can be sure of: they will thank you for it.

Your legs are the pillars that support your body and take you where your mind desires. Spoil them by paying attention to what you eat.

THE FEET

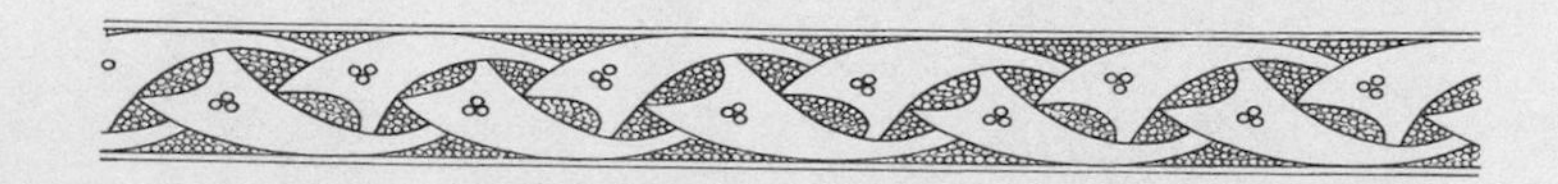

HOLD MY FEET, MOTHER AND GIVE ME STRENGTH

The secret of a correct position lies in the feet. A good foundation enables the whole body to find its space and the soul to unfold in harmony.
B.K.S. Iyengar

Your feet connect you to the ground, to the earth. When your soles rest on the floor and you balance your weight on both of them, then you can rest in yourself, you are in your center. With every step, you renew the contact and the connection to the earth, to matter, to *mater* the mother.

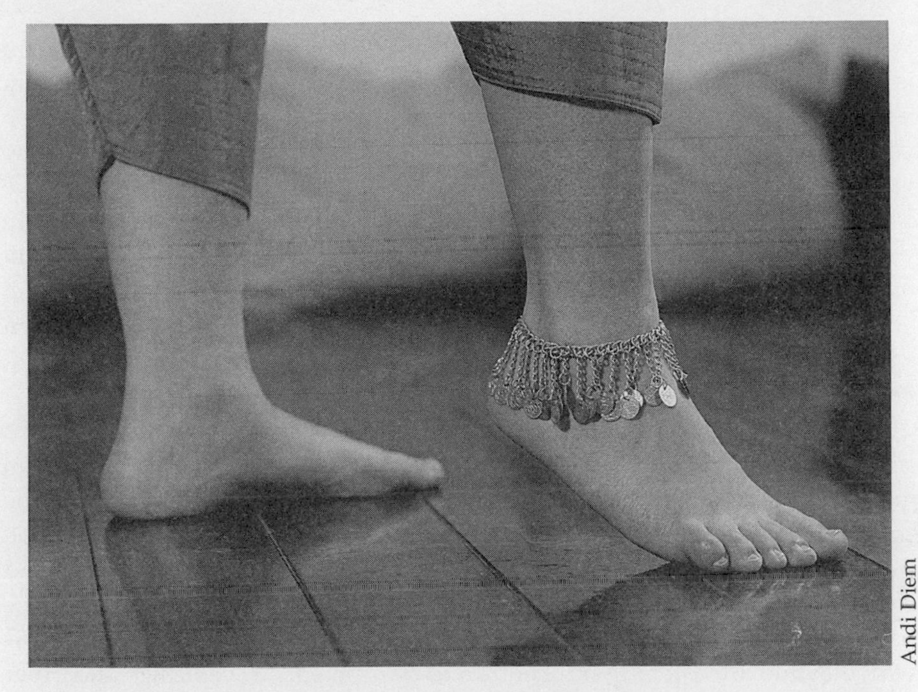

Andi Diem

Your feet reflect your balance...

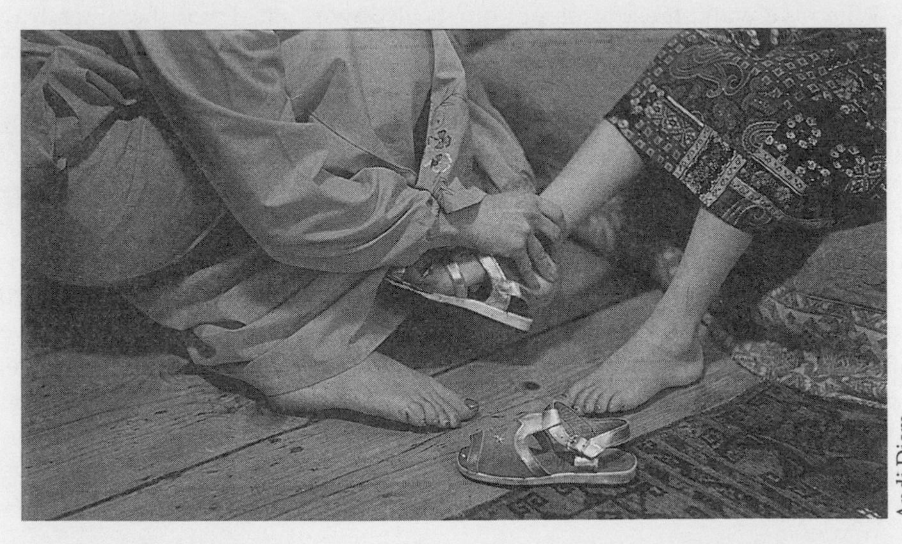

Andi Diem

...a balance you can pass along.

With every step, you massage all the organs of your body, because each organ is represented somewhere on your foot. This is why it is important to walk barefoot as often as you can, in order to awaken your whole body. So, when you dance, dance barefoot too, without shoes or socks, so that you may know where you stand and so that you may always replenish yourself with the strength of the earth. Let your toes, the balls of your feet, and your soles join in your dancing. Use your feet to stamp the floor, to stroke it gently and to walk on it with confidence. When you dance, stand on the balls of your feet, then let yourself drop on your whole sole—play with your feet! Always return from the vertical level to the horizontal one and let your feet make the connection between Heaven and Earth. Let your feet smile and enjoy your creativity.

In the East, special meaning is given to the feet and a human being's sensitivity can be told through them. The position of the feet is also given great care. This is why, for instance, when sitting, one will avoid turning the soles towards someone else or touching a valuable object with one's feet. Respect or apology is expressed toward an honorable person by bowing and either touching their feet with your hands, or kissing them. Just as with the hands, the sensitivity and the importance of the feet is well-known; this is why they too are colored with henna and pampered. At weddings and other important events in particular, one never forgets to dedicate oneself to this part of the body. Whenever one bathes, the soles and heels are rubbed with a stone, to keep them velvety and sensitive. The care people take of themselves can be told through their feet. No wonder that the feet are also seen as an erotic symbol.

When we walk, most of us put our heel down first. Try it the other way around, for a change, feeling your way first with your toes and the ball of your foot. Observe how your hips become more alert, how your rib-cage widens and how you experience every curve, how you become more aware of every change of the soil and of the earth. Native Americans learn to walk in this way when they are children, adapting themselves with every step to the surface they tread, so that they are able to creep up silently. Your body will thank you for this new inspiration and will show it through greater attention.

When you feel tired, when your head gets heavy and your connection to your body feels weak, sit down and give your feet a massage; take a little olive oil and knead your whole foot. Close your eyes and feel how every pressure, every stroke echoes throughout your body. Take time for your feet and, if you so wish, put on some music that you like, to help you relax. You'll see how, after such a massage, your feet will carry you on the floor in a more sensitive and more stimulating way. Above all... love thy feet as thyself!

Part Four: Variations and Rituals

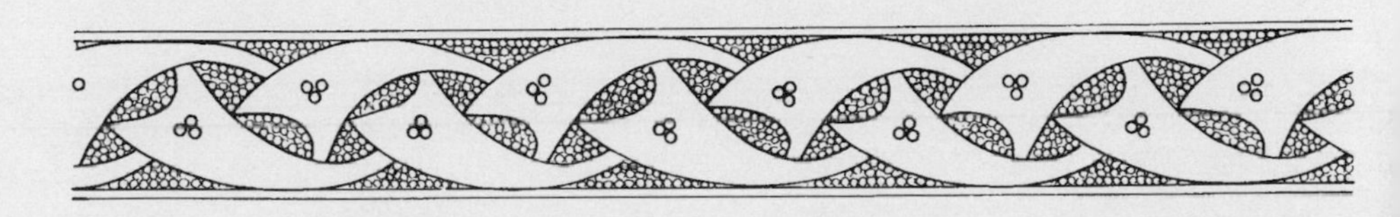

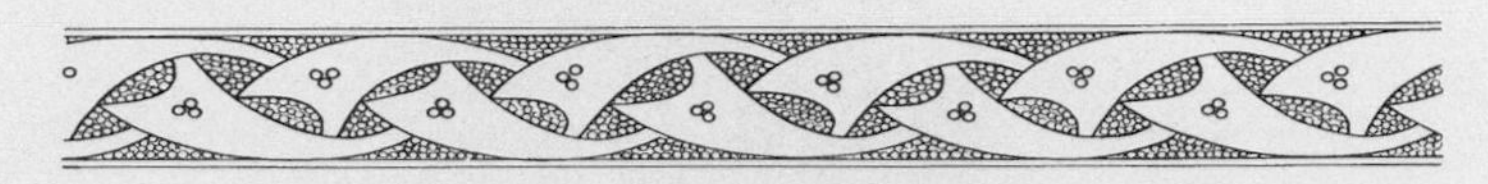

The Floor Dance

If you wish to elevate yourself, then you must learn to go to the ground...

It is in the floor dance that a woman's bond to the earth is expressed most strongly. The part of the body that is below the waist, namely the lap and the thighs, are given particular emphasis in this dance. The woman sits on the earth, owning and owned by it, her body center low to the ground. She is the queen who sits enthroned on the earth, from which she draws her strength. She is the quiet center out of which everything flows and to which everything returns.

Not using her legs makes the dancer's body blend completely with the earth. Everything happens as if the earth expressed itself through the dancer, inviting her to dance. By sitting on the earth, the dancer takes possession of the earth, and vice versa. The strength that a dancer draws from her belly is intensified through the close contact to the ground. Both thighs—that is, the dancer's lap—and the lower part of her body are emphasized in this dance, in which the Great Mother comes to the fore. In this dance, a woman expresses her close and loving relationship to the earth and reveals the awareness of life that makes everything born from the earth worthy of admiration. The dancer becomes the sister of the earth who awakens thoughts about the value of life.

In this dance, most movements are either performed with the dancer sitting on her knees or lying stretched on the earth. They are the same as those performed in a standing position, with the addition of nestling, rising up and sinking down, as well as embracing the earth.

When you perform the floor dance, you can use any of your favorite movements. If you lower yourself on your knees, then do it with the awareness

Holzknecht

The Floor Dance

of a queen who comes closer to her mother strength and finds her dignity inside herself. Anchor your energy in the ground and let it stretch all over you. You can use the floor dance to express feelings of melancholy, inner turmoil, lamentation, but also pride, power, and the mischievous feminine knowledge of maternal strength. All these feelings can find a particularly clear and beautiful expression through the floor dance.

There is a "feminine" Arabic prayer, for which one sits on the floor and says, "Blessed be the Lord! I cannot reach the sky and so I kiss the earth." When saying these words, the woman stretches her right hand as far as she can toward the sky and then she bends forward, touching the earth with both hands and kissing it, before kissing her hand and lifting it again to the sky.

Exercises

Lie on your back and observe yourself in this position, paying attention to all the parts of your body that are resting on the floor. Inhale deep into your belly and let all tensions and thoughts sink into the ground, into the earth. Observe your body as it relaxes more and more, your spine as it presses into the floor, your lower back getting closer to the ground, your neck and shoulders relaxing and sinking, your buttocks spreading, and your arms and hands getting heavier and more relaxed. The earth is draping its very skin over you. You are grounded. You have become part of the earth, swallowed by her gravity force like a child at its mother's breast. You are a hill in the landscape, a rock. Your strength springs from the earth and returns to it. Seasons come and go. Leaves fly over and away from you. Moss covers you, then silent snow. You grow tender buds and they unfold. Children run over you and depart and lovers lean against you. Gentle rain envelops you and you feel the warmth of the sun. You lie there, still yet full of life, life pulsing in you as you swallow the knowledge of centuries past and become the guardian of this knowledge, your belly filling up with history, and you lie there, eternal yet mortal, invisibly changing and rich throughout your being.

Now return to your body, let the blood flow and pump into all your limbs, stretch slowly and carefully, come back and open your eyes. How do you feel?

Let yourself fall to the ground, totally relaxed, calm, giving in to the weight of your body, to the force of gravity. Then come back up, majestic, showing yourself in all your pride and glory. And let yourself fall again, any odd way, and straighten up again. Repeat this game in which you play with the horizontal and vertical dimensions, until you understand that above and below, sinking deep and reaching high, flow from the same source, in the same way an hourglass is given an up and a down through the eyes of the beholder. Don't let yourself become influenced by language and by the value judgments implied in words; allow yourself to simply lend each dimension its own quality and meaning.

THE STICK DANCE

In this variation, belly dancing is performed with a stick, which is the dancer's outside partner and represents the male. In this way, the dance acquires a further dimension. The inner space, namely the dancer's body, is joined by the outer space, the male stick. The dancer plays with the stick, swirls it over

Andi Diem

The Stick Dance

her head, holds it up, and dances around it. She balances it on her shoulders, or on her head, holds it in both hands and moves it along her body in wave-like movements. She controls the stick and leads it as it pleases her. This is how she expresses her control over man as well as her partnership with him. She dances the masculine out of his mind, so that the woman's will may regain power. She shows this will and this force in a dancing, playful way. The force is not oppressive, but the self-confident, smiling, knowledge-treasuring expression of the feminine.

This dance was sometimes performed with a snake. The stick is connected to the snake in many cultures, and expresses the relationship between the feminine and the procreating male.

Patience and time are needed, until one can dance in harmony with a stick, uniting the softness of the body to the strength of the stick and creating out of both a new element. Yet, once this partnership has been achieved, it's great fun.

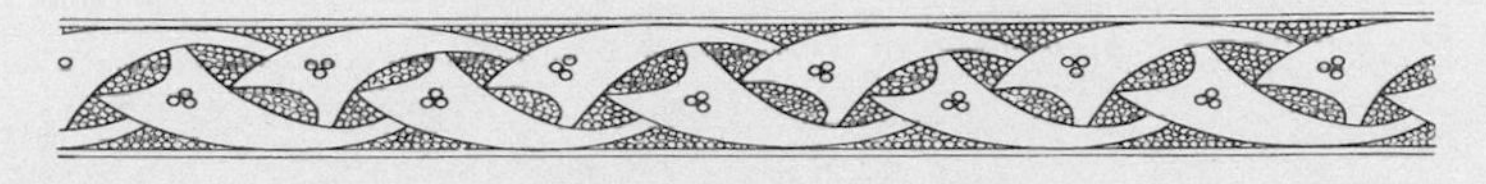

THE VEIL DANCE

The veil dance is a playful, erotic dance, in which the elements of reserve and openness, which make up the art of seduction, are expressed in a particularly beautiful way.

In many Islamic countries, women wear a veil. The veil was already common before Islam, especially in the region that has become Iran. It was not only meant to protect women from the sun, but also to raise the women of the upper social classes above those of the lower classes. The veil made them invisible; they could see without being seen. It enveloped them, lent them an aura of mystery, inviolability, and dignity. It conveyed their privilege over the lower classes, who could, as it were, be seen by everyone.

Wearing a veil, shrouding oneself, and covering one's head can be found nearly throughout the world in two periods of life: infancy and old age, at the beginning and at the end of the way. Is is possible that the head cover is used at these times to protect the head and hair from the outside, when self-protection is not yet, or no longer, strong enough? Or is the head thus covered because separation from the outer world and an introverted state are particularly important at these times?

In the Islamic world, veils and head covers are worn by women who have chosen the religious path and it is good that it is so. What is difficult to accept is that the veil should be made into a social constraint and that women may no longer decide themselves whether they are or are not ready for this.

In southern Iraq, especially in places of religious significance, all women, to this day, whether young or old, wear floor-length, black *abayas* over their clothes. Villages and cities are filled with these mysterious creatures. When you walk through the streets, similarly clad if you are a woman, you are overcome by an indescribable feeling of unity and solidarity with all the other women, regardless of age, appearance or social status; as if all belonged to a secret group from which men are excluded. The veil marks the limit between the world of men and the world of women. Women call each other sisters and this feeling of community gives one strength and confidence. How bare they appear, the men, sons of all these women! And the eyes, enhanced through those dark frames, shining and magnetic, seem to possess a hypnotic power and carry in them the whole energy and pride of these women.

A Veil Dance

No wonder that the veil is also used in the women's dance. It is fun to shroud oneself, showing only the part of oneself that one wishes to expose. The veil lends the dance an element of mystery. Swung over the head or over one's shoulder, it seems to take in the space and extend one's aura. As the dancer's body melds with the veil, the sacred manifests itself. The individual disappears behind the archetype, the divine; the mystical and erotic become one.

In the veil dance, a woman dances the knowledge of the new living creature that can be born from her. She dances the eternal return of life; even without children, she dances this awareness of life that comes to her from the rhythms inside. She dances Eros beyond the loving embrace; she dances the place in-between, the time between birth and death that is called life. By hiding and showing herself again, appearing and disappearing, seducing life and retreating, by being flirtatious and then proud again, erotic and then cheerful, indifferent and distant, exciting and shy as a child, she frees herself from external forms and abandons herself to the nature of things. She enters the world of unity. That is mystical Eros.

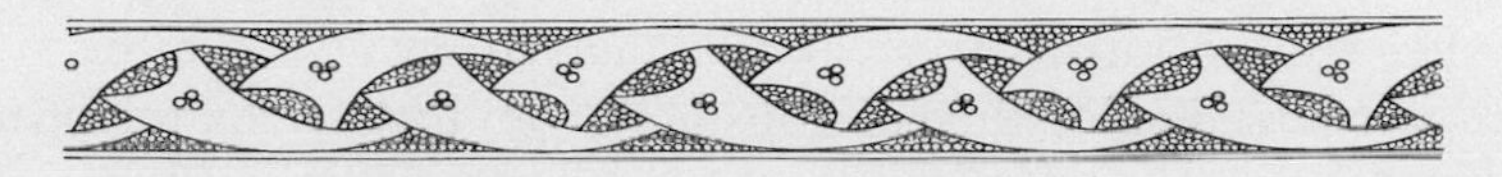

WALKING AND WHIRLING

Walking and whirling play an important part in belly dancing and its variations. Traditionally, all circles and whirls are performed counterclockwise; that is, toward the left. The left turn comes from the heart and lifts the woman from her earthy entrapment.

In Arab countries, small children are always carried on the left hip, close to the heart, so that they may be soothed by the carrier's heart beat.

When children are upset and would like to break up a friendship, they extend their left little finger and a turn of the left hand signifies the end of this friendship—until the next reconciliation.

In Islamic cultures, tasks are clearly divided between the left and the right hand. The right hand is for eating, writing and greeting, and the left hand for washing the genitals. This distinction is particularly strongly respected in water-deprived areas. The higher dignity of the right hand! It is interesting to note that all patriarchal civilizations favor the right hand. The right belongs to the masculine, active, natural power, which is creative, ruling, and spiritual.

And what about the left? When we examine ancient and prehistoric times in the Mediterranean regions, a central theme of similar characteristics and symbols comes to the fore: the left side was the mother's, the right side the father's; the left embodied the mortal, the right the heavenly world; left was matter, right was spirit; girls came from the left and boys from the right testicle; left the moon, right the sun; left night and right day; left rebellious and right willing; left space and right time; left simultaneous, right sequential; left even, right odd numbers.

In Plato's time, even numbers of animals were sacrified to the divinities of the earth, namely the ancient mother goddesses, whereas an odd number of animals were sacrificed to the new father divinities. Plato, the founder of patriarchy, was also the one who ascribed the right side to the gods and the left to demons.

At the time when matriarchy was still predominant in the Nile region, Isis's left hand was the nurturing and motherly one. Demeter carried her scepter in the left hand. Nike, the luck goddess, always stood on the left. In matriarchal cultures, female magicians and seers took their power from the left side of their body. In patriarchal cultures, power was linked to the right side of the body.

It seems that the older, matriarchal civilizations felt "the higher worth of the left side and an inner connection to matriarchy."[45] Were the symbols consciously reversed at the time of transition from matriarchy to patriarchy? In the eastern traditions, to this day, the left side of the body is said to be related to the feminine and receptive, as opposed to the right, active side of the body.

Why then is the right favored in patriarchal cultures? As we know, the right side of the cerebral cortex is connected to the left side of the body, while the left side controls the right side of the body. The right side of the brain is responsible for the creative, imaginative and intuitive processes of consciousness, while the left side is home to logical and analytical thought processes. Do we live in a world of right-handed people because of our left-brain orientation? Or are we left-brained as a result of our right-handedness?

In a dualistic society, in which the world is divided into good and bad, right and wrong, this value judgment has found a spatial expression: good is attributed to the right side and bad to the left. This principle also applied to the hands. Similar opinions and values are to be found on the linguistic level: right is correct and justified, while left is clumsy (as in the expression "to have two left feet") or even derogatory ("a left-handed compliment"). In Arabic, the word *usrawi*, left-handed, also means weak and dishonest.

In many cultures, the left hand is not given equal treatment and is distinctively less involved in various spheres of actvity. Right and left sides of the body are not subject to the same demands in terms of agility and grace of movement. Yet how is it possible to experience an unrestricted feeling of physical well-being when the body is only involved in part? Why not create with the whole body? There are many ways in which one can learn to use both sides of the brain and the body, to become more two-sided, thus benefitting, as it were, from both the matriarchal and patriarchal sides.

Exercises

Try once to write or paint with the hand that is not your dominant one. Start very relaxedly. You may feel a little impatient at the beginning. Go back to your childhood, to the first time when you picked up a pencil in your hand to fill a white piece of paper. Give free rein to your imagination! You will be surprised at how differently your non-dominant hand will proceed.

If you chose to write, you can start by writing your own name. Write everything down, all the feelings that come up about a favorite aspect or theme in your life. Do you feel like a child? Does this hand allow you to give more space to feelings and pictures? Do you notice any changes in your way of expressing yourself? Do you use different concepts from your familiar ones? Do you express yourself with greater emotions, sensitivity, in a more "right-brained" way? Could it be that, since most people are right-handed, the use of the right hand has resulted in a greater use of the left, rational, analytical nerve centers? Isn't it true that an organ that is regularly used is more strongly irrigated and therefore more developed? It has been established that the left side of the brain is heavier than the right.

Alternatively, you can start a dialogue between your two hands. Divide a sheet of paper in two by drawing a line in the middle and start painting or writing, first with one, then with the other hand. Now draw with both hands simultaneously. Let each hand draw its own, spontaneous picture. Let each hand perform its own dance. How does it feel and what does the picture look like? Compare and find out!

Choose activities that you would normally carry out with your dominant hand, and try to perform them with your other hand. Do not use your non-dominant hand for mere support, but give it the lead. You could also try alternating hands in any given activity. Observe yourself and the feelings that come up in this process.

In dancing, both sides of the body are fully involved and because belly dancing is a dance of isolation, not only are the demands placed equally on both sides, but you also learn to connect the various centers to the various structures in time and space. Nothing can have such a stimulating effect on both sides of the brain as this playful dance.

Holzknecht

WALKING

There are different ways of walking in belly dancing. The dancer uses them to switch from one rhythm to the next, and they also give her the possibility to rest a little and find new inspiration.

Basic Walk

Lean back a little, so that you leave as much space as possible for your hips. Imagine a ray of light coming out of your belly against which you hug your hips. Stand on the ball of your foot and walk through the room, "sitting in yourself."

Gazelle Walk

Stand with your feet in alignment. Take one step forward with your right foot, bend your knees, bring your left foot level with your right foot and stand on the ball of your left foot. Now take one step forward with your left leg, bend your left knee, bring your right foot level with the left, stand on the ball of your right foot, and so on.

Arabic Walk

In this walk, the footsteps are the same as when you walk normally. So: take a step forward with your right foot, bend your knees a little, turn your chest slightly to the right, then forward over the right foot. Now step forward with your left foot and bend your knees a little, while turning your chest to the left and forward over the left foot, and so on.

Stamping Walk

Use the same starting position as for the pelvis shimmy, namely with feet wider apart than usual. Go deep into your knees. While you swing your pelvis, shift your weight on to one foot and take one step forward with the other. Now shift your weight to that foot and bring the other level. You will need some practice and patience until you can perform both movements simultaneously. Whenever you feel that you have lost yourself in the two movements, always go back to the shimmy in the standing position. And don't forget: smiling is the best teacher!

Make sure that your upper body stays relaxed, that you don't pull your shoulders and that you keep your chest wide open. This is a wild, archaic walk, which is very impressive in its primitive way.

Camel Walk

In the camel walk, the upper body and the pelvis move together so that the

Andi Diem

whole body is shaped into a wave. Take the basic position and place your right leg forward, resting on the ball of the foot. The weight of the body is placed on the left foot which is flat on the floor. The right hand is placed on the temples, the left arm extended sideways. Bend your upper body forward. Breathe in, tense up your rib cage and lift it. The movement progresses to your buttocks, as you bend your knees a little and swing your pulled-back pelvis forward. At the same time, the weight of your body is shifted to the front leg and you bring the other leg level.

Swaying Walk

This walk is performed sideways. Place your left hand near the temple, like a flap, and extend your right arm out to the right, away from your body. Head and extended arm show the direction in which you will move.

Basic position: lift up your right hip (by stepping on the ball of your foot) and shift your weight to the left leg, take a small step tilted to the right side, shift your weight to the right foot and now lift your left hip, bring the left foot level and shift your weight to the left foot. And carry on sideways: right, left, right, left and so on. Once you have reached the end of the room, turn around and start in the other direction.

WHIRLING

Before you start whirling, it is essential that you be totally centered. Stand upright, bend your knees, close your eyes, and start circling with your pelvis.

And let me tell you a story: we divide the body into right and left sides. For most of us, one side is more developed than the other, more often than not the right side.

While you circle with your pelvis, thereby uniting both sides, look inside and listen. On which side do you rely more? On the left or on the right? Is it because it corresponds to you or because you were taught to rely more on that one? Take your time.

If you can't answer this question, keep observing. Try the following game: While your circle with your pelvis, which side of your head grows more hair? And how about your teeth? On which side do you usually bite, in which direction do you shift your food when you're chewing—left, right or both equally? And when you take the first step, do you entrust it to your right or to your left foot? Keep circling with your pelvis. How do your hands feel while you're circling? Which is your dominant, strongest, leading hand? And does it know about the other one? Pay attention to your ears. Which one seems to you most closely attached? Is one of your ears sharper? Now bring your attention to your feet and toes. How are you standing when you circle your pelvis? Keep circling, bring both sides into the "great circle." Take them both by the hand, as in a round dance. Keep circling until you become full and quite round. Then stop.

Use the information given by your body to look for your "neglected" side. Spend the rest of the day with it, get to know it, experiment with it, and observe your reactions, both inside and outside.

If you find that your right side, right hand, right foot and right hip are dominant, decide to use your left side today, and vice versa. Start by relinquishing your dominant side and play with the other. Write and cook with your left hand, bend forward to the left, carry things on your left side and step forward with your left foot. Rely exclusively today on your "weak" side. And don't forget to smile, on both sides!

The *Fatl* Whirl

The whirling dance of the dervishes can be incorporated in belly dancing. Extend your left arm horizontally, palm down. Lift your right arm with the palm directed towards the sky and tilt your head slightly to the right. Shift your weight to your left foot and make a circle with the ball of your right foot. In the dance of the dervishes, both soles are kept on the floor. You can, of course, also try this variation. The eyes are half-closed and look into the void. At the beginning, you may hold your right hand level with your eyes and look at it, if this makes it easier for you and gives you more poise.

The whirl is traditionally performed counter-clockwise, because all celestial bodies are thought to rotate to the left. You become embedded in their movement through your whirling. The leftward movement also helps you detach yourself from your connection to the earth and from yourself, in order to come closer to unity, the true aim of the dervish dance.

But the choice of direction remains entirely yours. Start slowly, without haste or stress. Before you can extend beyond yourself, you must first learn to know yourself.

Whirling can often lead to strong and unpleasant irritations of the inner ear, which provoke nausea and dizziness. This is one of the body's defense mechanisms, and it gives you a signal. According to how you feel, you may either give in and stop, or else try to overcome the blockage and limitation, and keep whirling. Do not see such blockages as something negative, for they are the path to knowledge. Do not hesitate to give into the force and gravity and let yourself fall. The earth will greet you like a mother. You may find it helpful to place your forehead on the ground in order to divert the dizziness or nausea.

If you wish to end the whirling, the *fatl* as it is called in Arabic—literally, winding, or rotating with—and you feel a little beside yourself, cross your arms on your chest, lower your chin to your chest and cross your feet and toes. The energy circle is thus fully closed. Remain in that position until you have "found" yourself again.

Egyptian Whirl

Extend your right arm and bring it up sideways, palm up. When you lower it, bring up your extended left arm sideways, palm up. Now start whirling while moving your arms as described above. This whirling can also be performed with a veil, whereby you hold both ends with your hands.

Half-Whirl

Extend both arms in front of your body, at shoulder level. Now bring your left leg forward and balance your weight on both legs. Use your right leg to rotate 180 degrees to find yourself in the same, mirror position, this time with your right leg forward. Practice several times until the movement flows, as if you were dancing with a partner. Once again, the invisible partner is yourself.

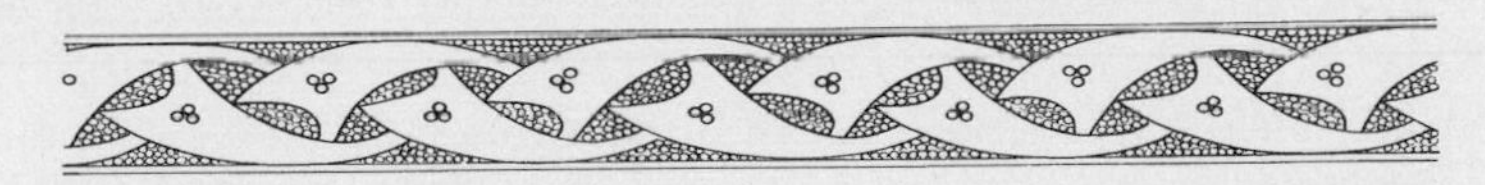

THE MENSTRUATION DANCE *(RAHIL)*

To this date, belly dancing has retained its ritual aspects in many Arab countries. It accompanies a woman throughout the phases of her life: menstruation, wedding, birth, death, taking on a different face according to each event.

The menstruation dance, or *rahil* (literally: awakening, departure) is an initiation dance. It is the gate entered by a young girl who comes out the other side as a woman. Women hold the gate open for her and through their presence, their cheers and their smiles, they lighten the young girl's passage to a new life.

When a young girl gets her first period, when she is "visited" for the first time, as they say in Arabic, this passage from childhood to womanhood is celebrated in many Arab countries by means of a ritual. All the women of the family, girlfriends, and female relatives congregate for this great event. A circle is made, the women hold hands and the girl (or, as the case may be, the girls) steps into the center of the circle.

It is customary in this ceremony for the hands and soles of the girl to be painted red with henna for the first time. The color red symbolizes, of course, the first menstrual blood, and therefore the young woman's ability to conceive and bear new life. Red stands for everything that is alive, birth as well as sacrifice, in the sense that something is sacrificed to make room for the new. The blood flows into the fertile, ever-pregnant earth, back to its origins just as through maturing, the young girl enters this state and finds her connection to the earth. Such is the meaning of the red color of her feet.

The women start moving softly and carefully. At the beginning, their movements are gentle and barely visible. One of the women asks the girl to address any questions that move her to the circle of women. She may ask anything, without shame or taboo, and the experienced women will answer her honestly. The women's rejoicing in their new companion and the girl's excitement are both carried by the circling movements of the women. The atmosphere is soft, full of strength and round as the pelvis of the women for whom this ceremony is also a gift that reminds them of their own childhood. Since the girl is considered to be particularly fragile and psychologically sensitive during this passage from childhood to womanhood, the circle of women protect her, guiding and safeguarding her with their knowledge. She must be carried safely into the world of women, where intuitive innocence blends with lively wildness and where a tender girl may grow to be a proud woman.

Above all, it is the women's sense of humor that helps the girl open up into this new phase of her life. Soon, two bowls are brought into the circle. One of them contains sweetened milk, which symbolizes virility, and the other dates, for femininity. One woman presents the girl with the milk. She takes a sip and then eats a date. This is repeated three times and the bowls are passed around the circle. The girl is offered both bowls as an encouragement to take care of the masculine and the feminine.

It is through this ceremony that little girls are admitted into the world of women, joyfull trills tearing apart the old world to make room for the new.

By now the room has filled with the women's wild, intense movements. Hips are circling strongly, arms moving in rhythm, and pelvises vibrating with all their might. Together, the women dance, sing, and laugh. At the end of the ceremony, the girl is congratulated and small gifts distributed. Then all the women eat and drink together, tidy everything up, and each of them returns to her own life.

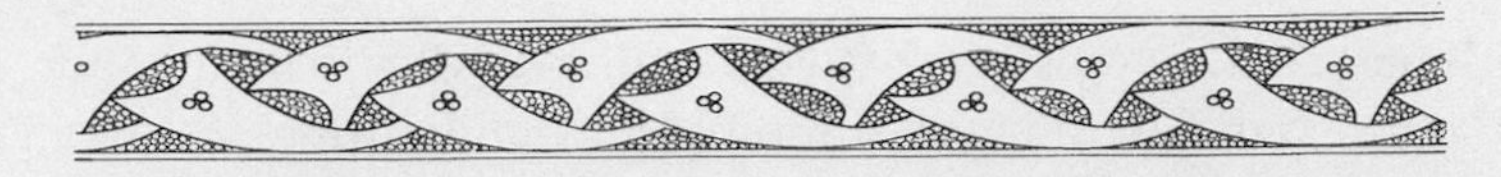

THE WEDDING DANCE

It is simply impossible to imagine an Arab wedding deprived of belly dancing. Belly dancing is the highlight of the wedding, though today it is usually performed by a professional dancer. Yet guests and relatives do not leave it at that; once everyone hears the music, they want to perform their own dance. Men and women both take part in this dance, accompanied by much enthusiastic clapping and singing by other guests. Dancers always give their best during these festivities, and at weddings the usual reserve in the presence of the other sex disappears.

To this day, wedding festivities vary from one country to the other, yet everywhere they stretch over several days. They consist of a men's day and a women's day, a women's henna day, and a prayer day. In this chapter, we shall first and foremost address the meaning of dancing during the wedding.

Traditionally, the wedding is celebrated separately by men and women. It is interesting to note that the wedding couple always stays with the women. The groom is thus invited into his bride's world. Most of the time, this will be his only opportunity, as an adult, to have a glimpse of this world. As a child, he lived, protected, in this world with his mother, until he joined his father's world. He now enters this women's world for the second time; this time, together with his wife-to-be.

Most of the time, the wedding couple sit majestically on an elevated stand, so that they may be seen by all. All the women perform belly dancing, each of them showing her skills, until the highlight: the bride's turn to dance. She dances for her husband for the first time. At this moment, all the women sit down, framing her dance like a picture. There is nothing shy about the bride's dance—she shows off the full bloom of her femininity to her husband and to the other women. Belly dancing gives her the opportunity to do so very directly, and it gives the husband a chance to discover his wife and appreciate her in all her womanly magnificence. Most of the time, the bride will leave the room several times—up to seven times—for a change of clothes and every time, her dancing will take on a different color and meaning. One may recall in this the dance of the seven veils and the meaning of the figure seven, which symbolizes the lunar cycle. Once the bride has completed her last dance, the other women stand up and dance with her. Lucky, the man who can thus be accompanied into his new life, and blessed is the woman who can thus be a woman.

In some countries, women then get up and leave the room with the bride.

The bride and all the women carry two burning candles in their hands. Slowly, carried by the sound of trilling, drumming, and tambourines, the women walk the bride back to her husband. Once they have arrived, they make a circle and each woman takes her light to the bride and dances with her. It is a soft dance, a gentle dance through which each woman gives the bride her blessing. The light, symbol of life and of the soul, is meant to illuminate the couple's common path. This procession of lights usually marks the end of the celebration and the wedded couple withdraw soon after.

At weddings, Bedouin women perform the hair dance, called *ni'isch*. Hair has always been considered by the Bedouins to be an erotic and feminine symbol. In this dance, the hair is rubbed with perfumed oils and swung from side to side through energetic movements of the head. The audience is made solely of women, who find themselves enveloped in this intoxicating scent. On such occasions, the men will usually peep through the folds of the tent, something of which the women are fully aware. It is often on such occasions that the next bride is chosen.

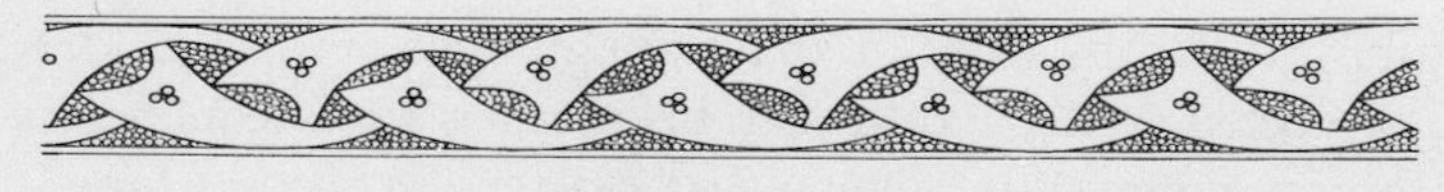

THE BIRTH DANCE

"...in ancient Asia, where dancing has retained its original purity,
it represents motherhood, the mystery of conception,
the suffering and the joy which accompany
the coming of a new soul into this world."
Armen Ohanian

The birth dance is not performed in all Arab countries. Yet, wherever found, it is one of the most impressive forms of dancing. No other dance expresses so strongly the strength and the longing of a woman for life and the overcoming of death. In this dance, the never ending return of coming and going, blossoming and fading away, finds its expression as well as the knowledge of the death that reaps every life.

To begin with, throughout pregnancy, belly dancing can play an important part. The movements of this dance form are particularly well-suited to prepare a woman for giving birth. In essence, belly dancing is a life and fertility dance, which fosters not only a woman's ability to conceive, but also helps her give life to a robust and healthy child. A woman's body is strengthened by this dance form, which also helps her to relax and give her baby the space needed to find its way out of her body.

Pregnancy and birth are natural processes. Women who have known and allowed themselves this experience, discover a new dimension of being, a deeper knowledge as well as a new confidence in their own abilities.

In order to improve one's understanding of the birth dance, it is important for it to be presented in a holistic way so that one may get to know the attitude of Arab women and Arab society with respect to pregnancy and birth.

The Time of Pregnancy

Once a woman has announced that she is pregnant, she is treated with special care. It is said that no pregnant woman's request may be denied.

Whenever the neighbors cook and they know that a pregnant woman lives nearby, they will take some of their food to her, so she will not smell it and grow an appetite she cannot satisfy. In so far as possible, the family tries to fulfill her wishes, because it is understood that any unpleasant mood of the mother-to-be could have an effect upon her child, both on a psychological and physical level.

In some families, the women are so provident that they will roast onions and garlic in olive oil, sesame oil, and butter and keep this mixture in the home. Should an appetizing smell come wafting in, the pregnant woman gets a little of this mixture to eat, or to rub into her navel, just in case the neighbors forget to bring something. At meal times, the women will always remember to leave the best pieces for the mother-to-be.

Certain activities should be shunned by the mother-to-be during her pregnancy: tasks that require her to squat or strain her back, and also tasks such as cutting, pulling up plants, or killing animals. Because of the new life growing inside her, a pregnant woman should not have to put an end to any form of life, for fear of adversely affecting the life growing inside her.

Precautions are also taken to ensure that no bad news comes to the ears of the mother-to-be. She should only see beautiful things and people, especially during the first six months, as the belief goes that this could influence the appearance of her child. Indeed, a mother-to-be is not only likely to wish for special food, she may also be overcome by powerful desires. Just by looking at someone, her child could come to resemble this person either physically or psychologically. This is why no one ever wonders why a child doesn't resemble anyone in the family, for one never knows who the mother may have seen during her pregnancy. Generally speaking, it is expected that the mother-to-be takes care of herself and that she pays heed to the advice generously dispensed by more experienced women.

The Child is Announced

In Arab countries, before birth was taken over by hospitals and doctors, it was exclusively a women's affair and, at least in part, it has remained so to this very day. A birth usually takes place in a specially prepared room. When the time comes, all men leave the house to take care of the father-to-be. Female relatives and neighbors ready themselves and gather in the birth-room. Pregnant women are not allowed to attend, as it is feared that their contractions might start prematurely. On the other hand, women who wish for children and have not yet succeeded, often like to attend so that they may somehow get infected!

Out of all the women who help the mother-to-be at the time of birth, great store is put in the presence of her mother. This reinforces the ancestral chain and reminds the daughter that once, her own mother too went through this experience. The mother sometimes comes from far away to be present at this great event; it is considered a very bad omen when she unable to do so. If need be, the pregnant woman will try to go to her mother's and have the child there.

Before going to a birth ceremony, all women perform a ritual washing similar to the one preceding prayers: they wash their hands, face and feet three times so as to achieve a state of spiritual and physical purity. A birth is felt to be sacred. Participating in a birth in a state of impurity could negatively influence its course.

To be allowed to participate in a birth is felt as a blessing; indeed the belief is that the birth-room fills with angels while the heavenly gates open above it. Every single wish and prayer can find its way directly to heaven, where it will, no doubt, be heeded.

The older women recite holy texts and help the mother-to-be to relax trustingly; others pray for her and utter prayers for protection. The room becomes filled with the women's soft voices. The pregnant woman is lulled into a state of absence and the pains become more bearable.

The midwife is usually an older, more mature woman who brings with her a vast life experience. She is often herself a mother already. Many women only want a woman who has already reached menopause, as it is believed that a woman's spirituality grows once she has left the menstruation cycles. The midwife sees to it that all women remain quiet and speak softly, because a woman giving birth is always in a state between life and death, a holy state of metamorphosis. Besides her skills on a physical level, the midwife's main duty is to protect the mother and infant from evil spirits and malevolent people and to secure their safety. This she achieves by means of whispered prayers for protection and rites that are passed on from one midwife to the next. Midwives often bring with them home-made medicines and herbs that are supposed to alleviate the pains of birth.

As soon as the intervals between the contractions shorten—the Arabic word for contractions is *talq*, literally, to be free, to be open—two stones and a little earth are brought. The earth is spread in front of the woman giving birth, so that it may absorb the blood and the waters, and return them to Mother Earth. One of the stones is for the mother-to-be, and the other for the midwife.

A hole is sometimes dug for the newborn child. When this cannot be done, a large dish is used instead and laid with furs or long towels. The women form a circle around the mother-to-be. They start singing in soft, low voices, while performing wave movements with their belly. These contraction movements resemble the belly's movements during labor. The soft movements are always accompanied by pulling and pushing the belly with a jerk. The mother-to-be will stand up and accompany the dancing women, before falling down again. The time of birth is a time of great transformation and the women's imitation of the birth movements is designed to help the mother-to-be as she opens to this overwhelming force. Her panting and groaning become embedded in the steady rhythm of the women whose presence and dancing take the mother-to-be into a state of trance, which helps her cope with the pain, transform it into strength, trust her body, and surrender. The pains she feels in the back and in the sacrum are assuaged through the rolling and circling of the pelvis, as well as through the gentle shaking of the hips. In this way, her body is better able to absorb, and then let go, of the pain.

Should the birth become protracted because the child is not in the proper position, four women will stand up. A carpet is brought and each of them takes one corner. The pregnant woman lies on it, to be shaken and rolled until the child has found the right position.

In the last phase of the contractions, the mother-to-be may choose among several positions. She may either place herself, supported by the other women, over the hole that will receive the newborn child, or she may squat, supported from behind, at the edge of the stone. A rope is sometimes fastened to the ceiling for her to hang on to. The baby is then received by the midwife and laid into the hole.

Sister Afterbirth

The baby is picked up by the midwife who wraps it in a towel. Now the time has come to wait for the afterbirth. Should it fail to come right away, one end of a piece of string is fastened to the umbilical cord and the other to the mother's big toe. As the mother stretches, the afterbirth is pulled out. She sometimes blows into a bottle to ease the process.

Another possibility is that the midwife will tie some towels around her head and press it against the mother's belly, until the afterbirth comes out.

In Arabic, the afterbirth is called "sister" and the midwife speaks to it tenderly while waiting for it. Once it has come out, it is wrapped and later buried—usually after having spent the night next to the newborn child—together with the earth that had been spread in front of the mother. Shortly after the birth, the mother's belly is either tightly bound or else massaged by an experienced woman so that the bones may resume their proper place. The child, wrapped and sometimes tied up, remains close to the mother who takes it immediately to her breast. The child is tied to protect it and strengthen its muscles. Soon after the birth, the mother is given unsweetened coffee and chicken soup.

When the child is born into a Muslim family, the midwife lifts it one last time up in the air and whispers into its ear the Islamic creed for the first time: "There is no God but Allah and Mohammed is his Messenger."

The midwife comes by every day for the first two weeks following the birth, to enquire about the mother and child. After the second week, her visits become less frequent, but she keeps coming until the first forty days are over. Throughout this time, the young mother will also be supported by the other women, until she has recovered her strength.

Welcome to Our World: The *Tulu'* Celebration

The situation changes after the fortieth day. Up until that day, mother and child are treated with particular care, as it is believed that they may still be in danger. The mother receives especially nutritious food and her female neighbors and relatives all take care of her. During that time, she is called *nafas*, which means "breath, respiration." Indeed, the belief is that she is still between life and death because her body has not yet fully "closed," her bones have not set back completely and the blood is still flowing. Sometimes she will still be massaged by an experienced woman throughout this phase.

After the fortieth day, she may move normally again, have sexual intercourse, attend prayers, resume her usual activities and—if it has been possible—leave the house only now. It is customary for this day to begin with a great washing ceremony.

In many countries, this is when a great celebration takes place in honor of the child. Only now is the child spoken to by name. This celebration is called *tulu'*, which means literally "coming out, going up, becoming visible."

The child is thus welcomed into and officially introduced to the community.

The Bedouins have a custom whereby the child is put on the outstretched legs of an old Bedouin woman known for her noble qualities, behind whom will stand several men, whether sons, uncles or brothers, since their presence is considered a sign of strength and prosperity. The child is blessed by the old woman and, should it be a girl, given her name. A boy receives either his grandfather's name or the name of a brave and respected man. A sword and a camel—today sometimes a jeep or an expensive car—are brought next to the child, to symbolize the courage, riches, and strength that should come to it in time. All eat and drink together before going their separate ways.

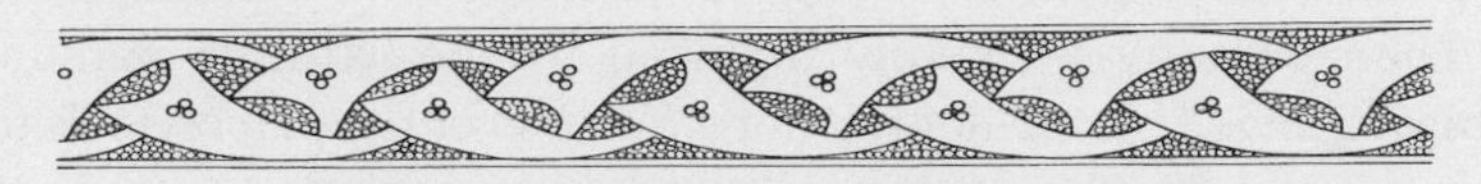

THE TRANCE DANCE

The trance dance is a ceremony that aims to heal a person, either on a spiritual or psychological level, of problems that may result from suppressed wishes or needs or from some socially-induced repression. These problems are seen as seated in the spirit; the idea is to heal and make the person whole again. Usually an old, experienced woman, who is either called *shaykha* (the old mistress) or *alima* (the one who knows) will lead such a ceremony. Special gifts of second sight are ascribed to her. She acts as the messenger between the ailing person and the spirits that have caused her sickness. She knows which spirit to summon, its preferences and the rhythm that will call it. Most of the time, she will beat this rhythm herself on the *daff*, the single-skinned, framed drum, which she holds vertically in her left hand and beats with her right hand. She shakes the drum and beats it against her body. Once she has fallen into a trance, it is through her that the spirit or *djinn* will state the wishes and conditions under which it will leave the patient and restore peace.

During the ceremony, the musicians perform various rhythms. When the right rhythm is heard, namely the one attuned to the ailing person's soul, she will stand up spontaneously and start dancing. Her head is usually covered with a piece of material, which prevents her from outside distractions. The trance dance is not a form of entertainment. Its sole aim is to heal the body and help the person. All people who partake in such a ceremony have the duty to support the "sick" person to the best of their abilities. Some will stand around her, supporting her in case she falls, or holding a corner of her clothes so that she knows that she is not alone and that all those present—relatives, friends and strangers—are standing behind her.

When the person falls into a trance, she throws the cloth away and the spirit that has caused the imbalance can be made to leave her. The spirit will usually ask for a sacrifice in the form of chickens or rabbits, which have been prepared in advance. The candle-lit room is clouded with incense. Flowers, nuts, fruit, and sweets are laid in dishes. The blood of the sacrificed animals is collected in a cup. The *shaykah* washes her hands in it and uses it to smear her face and that of the ailing person. The dancing becomes wilder. Those present may participate in it. When the *djinn* has left her body, the "sick" person usually collapses in exhaustion. The attendants hold her lovingly in their arms and sprinkle rose water over her, in order to bring her back to reality.

This ritual, reminiscent of old magical ceremonies, may extend over several hours. The ceremony is usually financed by the "ailing" person and is sometimes followed by smaller reunions. Whenever the person feels the need, she returns to the *shaykha*.

Such ceremonies have survived to this day in North Africa and in other Arab countries. They vary somewhat in terms of sequence, intensity and timing—some are only performed during the day after sunrise, others only after sunset. Yet, by and large, they resemble each other and are most popular among women. In Egypt, they go by the name of *zaar*; in Algeria, they are called *jarjabous* in Tunisia, *stimbali*. In Morocco, they are mainly performed by the tribe of the Gnawas, who claim Ethiopia as their country of origin. In those ceremonies, the musical instruments, the movements of the lead dancers, and the color of their clothes all play an important role. The sacrificial animal, usually a lamb, has been killed in advance. At the beginning of the ceremony, it is shared by all the guests together with rice mixed with raisins and prunes, unleavened bread, and yoghurt. Then the music starts and the lead dancers begin their ritual dancing, in which each movement has a special meaning.

During the dance, each dancer is covered with a special colored garment, following a predetermined sequence. The color that corresponds to each dancer and the particular rhythm that makes him or her get up and dance are indications of his or her state of trance. In this way, black is the color of the earth spirits, red of the fire spirits, white the air, and blue the water spirits. While in the trance, some people cut themselves with knives, or draw swords through their abdomens. Amazingly enough, no wounds are ever seen after such ceremonies.

The most important aim of the trance is to free oneself of negative emotions and depressions. Trances may also be used, however, to "process" disasters such as miscarriages or accidents. One may also begin such a ceremony with an unfulfilled wish, in the hope that a transformation may follow the "purification." As is true of most trance dances, the Gnawas do not usually separate the sexes for these ceremonies. It is the soul that is central to the healing, so everyone participates, whether as helpers or as conjurers. Trance dances performed from sunset to dawn are always led by a master, while those beginning at sunrise are led by a mistress, a *lalla*.

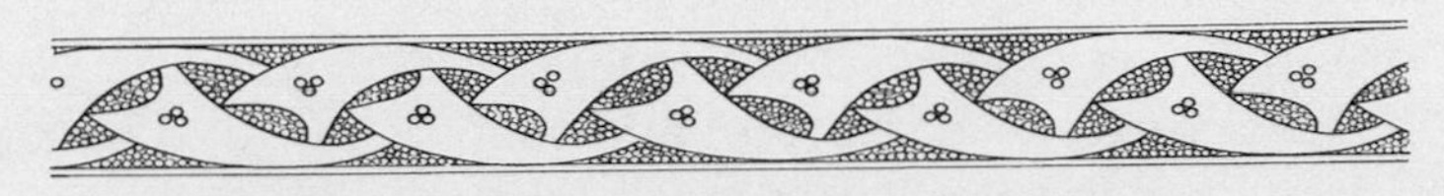

THE MOURNING DANCE

We are born out of a woman's belly and to the belly of the earth we return. When our beloved ones leave us, the pain and emptiness that follow in their wake can be so overwhelming as to become unbearable and crush our hearts. Body and spirit are so saturated with pain that everything is like one big wound. To divert the pain, the body spontaneously falls into a monotonous movement, with the trunk going forward and backward continuously. I have often seen women, standing at the grave of a beloved one, move their body forward and backward imperceptibly, just as do some praying people, or the so-called insane. The rocking movement leads them into the black and blue mourning trance, their faces shut from the world by a veil of tears, their eyes looking inside.

Sitting on the earth, they move their upper bodies quietly, circling in their middle. From the belly of life, their voices carry their wailing to the sky. Gazing inward, they dig the pain from the depth of their souls and express it through their bodies. They fall on their knees and the movement extends to their circling upper body. Along some invisible spiral, they descend into the world of the departed, rising up again to dig their nails into the earth, as if to bring back their beloved ones. Out of the pain of their soul, soft sobbing, whining and groaning rise from the deep cave of their bellies. Time and again, women gather to bear the mourning through the circling of their joined bodies. In this fashion, each woman becomes the cup that receives the other's woe and agony. Time and again, the earth is awakened to a new life through the moisture of their tears; through the gentle movements of life, the women defy death, and thus carry the souls of the dead gently into another world of existence.

The mourners are accompanied completely and entirely in their grief for three days and three nights. All pain, down to the deepest rooms of the soul, must be poured out and experienced without restraint. No tears must be held back, no lament or scream stifled. Only in this way may the soul rise up again, purified through the salty tears. Throughout this period, the mourners are never left alone and they are not involved in any work. In the following days, there is always someone close by, and only slowly do they resume their usual activities.

Departure and loss are always linked to pain; and it need not be the loss of a beloved one. Every transformation in the life of a human being demands that the past becomes dead; the pain and the grief are the bridge that leads to the new, over the river of fear. This mourning dance, which I call a dance because the whole person—body, spirit and soul—is called to partake in it, helps one move beyond the limitations of one's own pain and offers a consolation that reaches from the depth of the individual to the higher level of understanding Unity.

So dance, sister: keep dancing for life, keep dancing against death. Cry and know that we share your grief through every one of your tears.

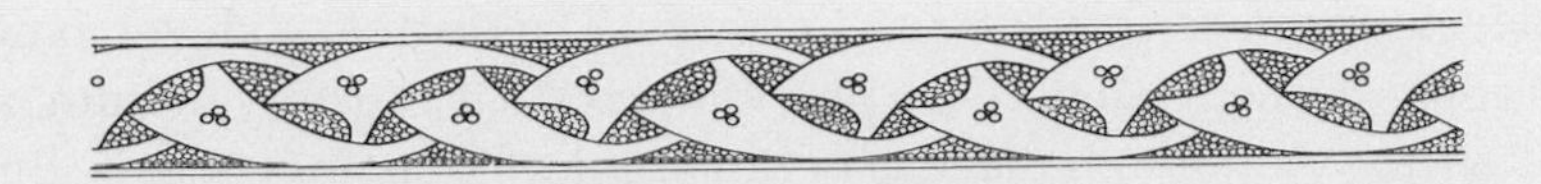

EPILOGUE

The dances and rituals described in this book are meant to inspire and maybe lead women to build their own rituals into their lives. For instance, marriage rituals are found in all societies, regardless of social class; but how about divorce rituals, a way of marking the decision of two people to revert to their separate ways? At a time when such separations are more frequent than in the past, perhaps because people are less ready to compromise, perhpas because economical dependence is no longer an obstacle, rituals should also be adapted to the new circumstances. And how about rituals for our young? What initiations can we give them to help them find their way and connect to their inner strength?

We live in hectic and loud times, when the voice and the dignity of the individual often remain unheeded and ignored and where loneliness is the price we pay for that. Why not examine the customs of other cultures to inspire us with new forms and help us fight the dehumanizing processes of our own cultures?

When I look at the women in the two cultures known to me, Arab and Western, in one of them I see a woman, fully aware of her femininity, yet only allowed to experience it within a pre-defined frame and with no possibility to live her masculine side. In the other, I see an active woman who stands on her own two feet and plays down her femininity in an honest attempt to be taken seriously.

Look over and above, sister, and don't let prejudice hamper your inspiration, your creativity, and your actions!

The written history is masculine and it tells us about the conquests, wars, achievements, victories, and defeats—in other words, it tells us about power.

Time and space are shaped and marked through external events. Human development and evolution are measured by the yardstick of these events.

So far history has been presented to us as a linear development, from prehistorical to modern times, through antiquity and the Middle Ages, with European-Christian history considered to be the highest human development.

This naive and archaic historical representation can lead to a discriminatory attitude, insofar as it considers all previous or parallel developments to be inferior. This is a superficial view which overlooks one major aspect of human life.

Outer development can only be measured against inner development. This inner development relates to consciousness. The degree of development of human consciousness is a decisive phenomenon in the history of humanity. If we look at history through the lens of human development—that is, through the lens of the development of consciousness, it no longer appears to be a straight line or chain, in which the individual parts are assessed according to their place. Instead of the line there appears a unity that treasures individual cultures and sees them as enriching. In this way, the many different cultures, religions, and attitudes to life exist next to each other and inspire one other; a family of human beings, in which individuals are sources of mutual inspiration, who may further the development of consciousness among all human beings.

There are more people on this earth than ever before. The technical possibilities of media and transportation have moved us so close together that we can exchange information and reports in unbelievably short time. In theory, this has enriched us and could lead to greater understanding among us human beings, to mutual enrichment and growth. But this can only happen provided we respect the diversity of cultures and ways of life, treasuring their «otherness» for its own sake, without judgment. Sometimes understanding and reflection require so much effort that it is easier to judge. Unfortunately, the kind of linear attitude usually involved in making judgments can easily lead to uniformity, to the absorption of other forms of existence, and to contempt for other cultures. It would be as if we destroyed the multicolored variety of flowers in earth's garden, reducing them to a single species, only to tire of it.

A new awareness must grow among human beings; an awareness that acknowledges our unity, our existence as one living organism, ever changing and mutating, each part benefitting from and stimulated by the other. When we speak of a unity, a whole, we do not mean uniformity, but sameness in its manifold manifestations. Human beings are the same in that each one of us longs for life, for the meaning of life. But each one of us, embedded in our own culture and our own life space, gives this search and this longing a different shape and offers a different view, a different solution. Who can say that the elephant is more splendid than the ant? And who can say one person's view is more valuable than another's? As long as we stay firmly in our own position in the human circle, we make assumptions, while the mystery sits in the middle and knows. A famous Arab tale illustrates this idea.

One night, it was announced that a totally new being had been caught, a creature that had never been seen before. It was being kept in a tent. Such was the villagers' curiosity that they couldn't wait until the next morning. There was no moon in the sky and the night was pitch black. Four villagers crept under the tent; each of them touched the animal in a different place. One touched it and said, "This creature is like a big, fluttering butterfly!" Another, touching elsewhere, declared, "It's like a giant worm!" The third villager touched yet another place and muttered, "It's as big and heavy as a tree trunk!" The fourth, having touched yet another part, was convinced that it looked like a broom. They stole away and related their impressions to the rest of the villagers. Convinced of his own description, each was indignant and mad at the others' inaccuracy. They argued and called each other liars. A wise old man broke the discussion by saying "Let us wait until tomorrow, when we can see this being!" By the next dawn, everyone had already gathered and were waiting impatiently outside the tent. As the animal was brought out, a great "Aaah!" went through the crowd and all laughed happily. "It's like a butterfly, but only in part!" "It's like a worm, but only in part!" "It's like a tree trunk, but only part of it!" "It's like a broom, but only part of it!" "You were right, all of you," said the wise old man, "but only in part. Together your partial knowledge becomes greater, and you understand!" The animal that could now be seen by all was an elephant...

We live in times ruled by traumas and tensions which call for a new order for the kind of understanding these villagers achieve only when they all come together.

In one half of the world, humans starve for food and are so weakened that they can barely raise their heads to acknowledge other dimensions. Yet, strangely enough, more faith and trust are to be found in that part of the world than in the other. The belief that there is a predestined way for everyone lifts people over their worries and beyond materialism. It puts them in a state of expectation and acceptance that stimulates the gift and the art of letting go and letting flow, of seeing the divine light behind all things. In the East, the soul learns to fly, but the body is utterly exhausted by life circumstances. Faith helps people grow beyond their short span of life. To them, "life" is not limited by birth and death, but exists in other forms before and after; life on earth is but one segment of existence. The pressure of time disappears, life becomes easier and more flowing and one can accept everything more patiently. This may also be why one feels grateful for the small things in life, since nothing is ever taken for granted. Yet in this process, one often forgets to question and use one's own creativity and strength, and the skill of action and free choice is restricted. Because without one's own strength and knowledge, one cannot find oneself.

The other half of the world starves for faith, trust and spirituality. Health, vitality, prestige, wealth, and success are the norm. The individual is everything and needs no one but him or herself. The skills of self-sufficiency are well taught and have helped many people grow and develop. But human growth lies in the combination of both: to learn through the tools that people have developed and also to understand that they are embedded in the Great Soul; to grow over their own egos and connect with the laws behind the universe; to find their own way and to trust, too. And is love not the key that unites the inner and outer worlds?

In the West, classification, consumption, pleasure, and entertainment seem to rule our lives. Reason is highly praised, while feelings from the belly mostly repressed. For most people, humanity only comprises their own children, close relatives, and good friends. Their fellow citizens are strangers, however close they may physically be; one does not see them or come in contact with them. People live in small, fabricated worlds, strangers among strangers; the only thing they have in common is their love of public peace and their fear of all change. Many have no idea where they stand in life and in relation to themselves. To feel responsible for and at peace with one's neighbor, to feel respect—are feelings and concepts that have no place in this system. Does that mean that love too has no place here?

As Erich Fromm put it so aptly, "Love means that we give ourselves to the other without guarantee, that we abandon ourselves totally to the ones we love in the hope that our love will awaken love in them too."[46]

To learn to know oneself is the basis of all understanding and love. The "dance around the self"—which should not be allowed to degenerate into misunderstood narcissism—can lead to inner wisdom.

Inner spiritual growth and intelligence are the two hands that hold the heart and make it expand and understand the treasures and miracles of life. True knowledge is based on the combination of these three sources, from which self understanding can blossom. Reality is based on one's inner state and mirrors outer understanding.

When we find unity within ourselves, everything around us answers us, not least nature. If our world were peopled by such beings of unity, it would be our paradise.

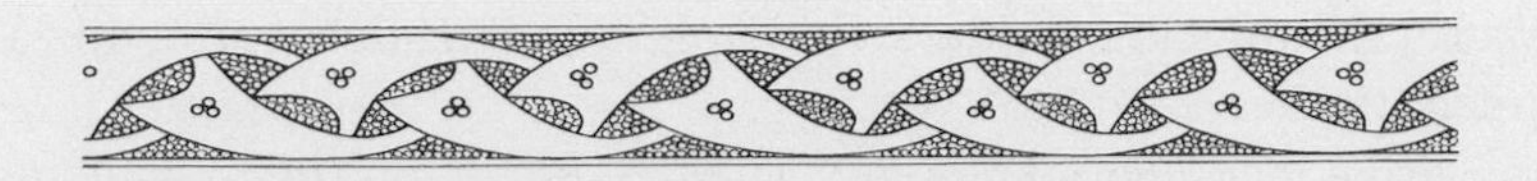

Works Cited

Bachofen, Johann J. *Complete Works, Vol II.* Basle, 1948.

Behrendt, Joachim Ernst. *Muscheln in meinem Ohr. Hörspiel* (Mussels in my ear). Radio play.

Bornemann, Ernest. *Das Patriarchat. Ursprung und Geschichte unseres Gesellschaftssystems.* (Patriarchy: Origins and history of our social system). Frankfurt am Main, 1991.

Borst, Arno: *Lebensformen im Mittelalter* (Forms of life in the Middle Ages). Frankfurt am Main, 1979.

Brunner, Otto. "Vom 'ganzen' Haus zur 'Familie'" (From the "whole" house to the "family") *Seminar: Familie und Gesellschaft-sstrucktur*. Frankfurt am Main, 1978.

Buonaventura, Wendy. *Serpent of the Nile: Women and Dance in the Arab World.* New York: Interlink Books, 1994.

Cahen, Claude. *Der Islam.* Frankfurt am Main, 1982.

Capacchione, Lucia. *Die Kraft der anderen Hand* (The strength of the other hand). Munich, 1990.

Chishti, Shaykh Hakim Moinuddin. *The Book of Sufi Healing*. New York, 1985.

Dhondt, Jan. *Das frühe Mittelalter* (The early Middle Ages). Frankfurt am Main, 1995.

Estés, Clarissa Pinkola. *Women Who Run with the Wolves: Myths and Stories of the Wild Woman Archetype.* New York: Ballantine, 1993.

Feldenkrais, Moshe. *Das starke Selbst* (The strong self). Zurich, 1989.

French, Marilyn. *Beyond Power: On Women, Men and Morals*. New York: Ballantine, 1988.

Fromm, Erich. *Die Kunst des Liebens (*The art of loving). Berlin, 1980.
Ghazal, Eluan. *Der heilige Tanz. Orien talischer Tanz und sakrale Erotik* (The sacred dance: Oriental dancing and sacred erotism). Berlin, 1993.
Gleede, Edmund. "...ich empfinde Menschen stark" (I sense people strongly). Gleede speaks with the head of the Wuppertal Ballet. In *Ballett 1975: Chronik und Bilanz eines Ballettjahres* (Ballet: Chronicle of a year of ballet). Velber bei Hannover, 1976.
Göttner-Abendroth, Heide. *Für die Musen. Neun Essays* (For the muses: Nine essays). Frankfurt am Main, 1990.
Göttner-Abendroth, Heide. *Die tanzende Göttin. Prinzipien einer matriarchalen Ästhetik* (The dancing goddess: Principles of matriarchal aesthetics). Munich, 1982.
Hegers, Ulrike. *Bauchtanz. Frauen finden ihren Rhythmus* (Belly dancing: Women find their rhythm). Düsseldorf, 1991.
Ichazo, Oscar. *Lebenskraft aus der Mitte* (Life force from the middle). Munich, 1990.
Klein, Gabriele. *FrauenKörperTanz. Eine Zivilisationsgeschichte des Tanzes* (WomenBodyDance: A civilization's history of dancing). Berlin, 1994.
Neumann, Erich. *Die große Mutter* (The great mother). Olten, 1974.
Sachs, Curt. *Eine Weltgeschichte des Tanzes* (A history of world dance). Hildesheim, New York, 1976.
Schmimmel, Annemarie. *Mystische Dimensionen des Islam* (Mystical dimensions of Islam). Köln, 1985.
Servos, Norbert. "Tanz-Lust oder Totentanz?" (Life dance or death dance? Reflections on the freedom of movement in dancing). In *Ballet International* 12:7/8.
al-Shaduli, Shaykh Muhammad al-Jamal al-Rifai. *Fruits from the Tree of Life.* Santa Fe, 1995.
Touma, Habib Hassan. *Die Musik der Araber* (The music of the Arabs). Amsterdam, 1975.
York, Ute. *Mondstrahlen. Ein praktischer Ratgeber zur Nutzung der geheimnisvollen Kräfte des Mondes.* (Moonshine: A practical guide to using the mysterious forces of the moon). Munich, 1993.

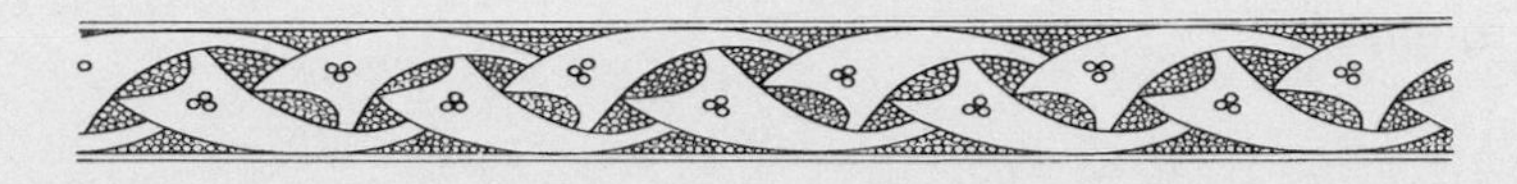

End Notes

PART II: A History of Women's Dance

[1] Göttner-Abendroth, *Dancing* 45+.
[2] Göttner-Abendroth, *Muses* 103-104.
[3] York 156.
[4] York 159.
[5] See Neumann 167.
[6] York 303.
[7] York 159.
[8] Klein 23.
[9] Sachs 166.
[10] Klein 38.
[11] Klein 44.
[12] See Dhondt 9.
[13] Borst 70.
[14] Borst 71.
[15] Borst 71.
[16] Klein 57.
[17] See Buonaventura 38.
[18] See Buonaventura 94.
[19] Klein 65.
[20] French 260.
[21] Klein 71.
[22] Klein 128.
[23] Brunner 89.

[24] Klein 87.
[25] Klein 81
[26] Klein 165
[27] Gleede.
[28] Servos 33.
[29] Klein 268.
[30] Hegers 22.
[31] Hegers 26-27
[32] Fromm 140.
[33] Estés 122.
[34] Fromm 11.

Part III: From Head to Toe

[35] See Feldenkrais 135.
[36] Touma 57-58.
[37] Touma 59.
[38] Behrendt extracts.
[39] Schimmel 16.
[40] Cahen 272.
[41] The descriptions provided here refer to the work cited by Chishti as well as to the oral statements of Shaykh Muhammad Al-Jamal Al-Rifal Al-Shaduli.
[42] See Ichazo 75.
[43] See also the sensitive explanations in Ghazal 79.
[44] Feldenkrais 266.

Part IV: Variations and Rituals

[45] Bachofen 18.
[46] Fromm 140.